reading aids series

MAKING
SENSE reading comprehension improved through categorizing

Christian Gerhard
Prince George's County Public Schools
Maryland

Review Editor   Helen J. James

An Service Bulletin

INTERNATIONAL READING ASSOCIATION • Newark, Delaware 19711

Copyright 1975 by the
International Reading Association, Inc.

Library of Congress Cataloging in Publication Data

Gerhard, Christian.
    Making sense.

    Bibliography: p.
    1. Reading comprehension. I. Title.
LB1050. 45.G47   428'.4'3   75-37706
ISBN 0-87207-218-5

Second Printing, May 1977

Contents

Foreword *vii*

Introduction *viii*

1 Chapter One GETTING READY

4 □ What is categorizing and what is the role of the senses in categorizing?
　　　Sorting or grouping after careful observation *5*
　　　Recognizing common characteristics *5*
　　　Labeling according to common characteristics *6*
6 □ Why does everyone categorize?
　　　Categorizing for survival *7*
　　　Categorizing for efficiency and prediction *7*
9 □ How does categorizing help people to learn and to remember?

15 Chapter Two SOME DIFFERENT WAYS OF CATEGORIZING

16 □ Can an object be categorized in different ways?
17 □ Is there a need to observe carefully in order to categorize well?
17 □ What are some ways in which one can categorize?
18 □ Is there a difference between form and function?
18 □ Can the same object perform different functions?
21 □ Is it important to know many different ways of categorizing for solving problems?

25 Chapter Three CATEGORIZING OF OBJECTS LEADING TO SENTENCE WRITING

28 □ Can different ways of categorizing be demonstrated with actual objects?
30 □ How can categorizing lead to sentence writing?
32 □ Is there a possible relationship between a category and a paragraph?

37 Chapter Four THINKING IN CATEGORIES

39 □ Can all kinds of items besides objects be categorized?
39 □ What are some other ways of using categories?
　　　Comparing and contrasting *40*
　　　Positive and negative views *41*
　　　Vocabulary study *43*
　　　Finding categories in reading material *46*
47 □ What are some of the dangers of categorizing?
　　　Prejudice *47*
　　　Poor judgment *47*

49 ☐ Can any category be used to build a paragraph? Must all paragraphs be built this way?

49 ☐ Can a category be broken into other categories?
  Hierarchies 49
  Relationships 51

55 ☐ Can many categories be related in written units larger than a paragraph?

59 Chapter Five WRITING TOPIC SENTENCES

61 ☐ What are the two parts of a sentence?
62 ☐ What is the purpose of a topic sentence?
63 ☐ What are the important requirements of a topic sentence?
65 ☐ What are the parts of a topic sentence?
68 ☐ What role does style play in written language?

70 Chapter Six COMPLETING PARAGRAPHS FROM SPECIFIC ITEMS OF CATEGORIES

71 ☐ Can specific items of a category be used for completing a paragraph after the topic sentence has been written?
71 ☐ How are the specific items chosen?
73 ☐ What do we mean by logical order?
  Chronological order 74
  Geographical order 75
  Sequence 75
  Cause and effect 75

80 Chapter Seven COLLECTING AND ORGANIZING IDEAS FOR WRITING

81 ☐ Are there reliable ways of collecting ideas for writing?
  Using association of ideas 81
  Tapping personal experience 82
  Using sense impressions 82
  Using emotions 83
  Using or interpreting symbols 83
  Using different meanings of words 83
  Comparing and contrasting 84
  Thinking about cause and effect 84
  Doing research 84
  Brainstorming 85
87 ☐ How can ideas be organized for writing?
88 ☐ What is the purpose of having an introduction and a conclusion?
  Writing an introduction 89
  Writing a conclusion 89

94 Chapter Eight WRITING A BRIEF ESSAY

95 ☐ Is a systematic approach to writing tasks possible?
96 ☐ Why has a short essay been chosen as the form, or *product*, culminating the categorizing exercises?
97 ☐ Why is it important to understand the *process* of gathering, organizing, and writing down ideas?

iv

98 ☐ Why will students get eight separate grades for completing the essay?

98 ☐ Why is it important to keep all worksheets until the eight steps have been completed?

Choosing a topic *99*

Organizing ideas in categories *99*

100 ☐ Why is it important to follow paragraph form?

104 ☐ Does learning a process for organizing ideas help people to read more intelligently?

110 Chapter Nine APPLYING THE CATEGORIZING PROCESS TO READING: BUILDING ADDITIONAL THINKING SKILLS

117 ☐ How can the previously described system of collecting and organizing ideas be used to understand how other writers have organized their ideas?

Previewing for reading *118*

Reading for meaning *121*

128 ☐ What reinforcement activities are essential in order to assure retention and use of this system for both reading and writing?

Writing paragraphs *128*

Turning paragraphs into categories *129*

Reading and writing related to practical tasks *129*

131 ☐ Can other aspects of language development and usage be incorporated into this system as aids to better reading and writing?

Conjunctions and sentence structure *131*

Adverbs and prepositions *135*

135 ☐ Can students derive other systems of organization from a thorough understanding of how categories are built and used in reading and writing?

Cause and effect statements *136*

Conditional statements *137*

Alternation statements *138*

Negative statements *139*

Review *141*

Continuing ways to improve reading *143*

Previewing *143*

Peer teaching *144*

Parent help *144*

Student glossary *148*

Bibliography *160*

ACKNOWLEDGMENTS

To Alma Morris go special thanks for being the first to stimulate the author's interest in the problems of reading.

Grateful acknowledgment is extended to Helen J. James, who served as review editor of this volume. Dr. James' broad background of teaching and reading experiences, her encouragement and enthusiasm for this project, and her professional assistance sustained the author throughout the development of the manuscript.

Many valuable comments and helpful suggestions were contributed by Sue M. Brett, Jack Carr, Beth Davey, Louise Waynant, and Joan Adams. Special recognition is offered, in addition, to Joan Righter and to other classroom teachers who took on extra work and were willing to try the new procedures described in this book. Work with these teachers led to the development of many practical approaches offered in the program.

Foreword

Education is, and must be, a process of enabling learners at all levels to "make sense" of their worlds of reality. An influential element in processing that world is the act of reading; and learning how to read is an essential step in the process. Making sense of reading, then, becomes a significant activity. As such, it is the goal of this book.

With the patience and resolve of many effective teachers, Christian Gerhard searched for a threshold of "making sense" experiences to stimulate clearer thinking in middle-school learners. Detailed records of procedures were kept and when an effective format had been created other teachers were invited to try the techniques. This volume is the result of several years of rigorous evaluation and refinement.

Recognizing the great value of adequate concepts in reading and writing tasks, Gerhard applied Piagetian techniques to improve learners' *conscious* processes of conceptualization, beginning at a concrete level. By alternating oral language and written language experiences, skills-training episodes were devised that not only met learners' needs but also released creative talents. With intuitive and practical judgment, learner interaction and small-group activities were utilized to sustain open-ended and divergent thinking, yet accurate and adequate categorizations. The provision of models and self-checking techniques maintained the necessary teacher guidance and immediate reinforcement to assure success.

This presentation is a sincere endeavor to develop clear understandings of the interrelatedness of oral/written experiences and reading/writing processes that lead to making sense of reading. Teachers, regardless of subject-matter interest or grade level or preferred teaching style, will discover something of value in the logical, useful instructional suggestions offered here.

It may be that Gerhard provides an important missing instructional link which educators have been seeking. This volume may serve as a vital complement to George H. Henry's *Teaching Reading As Concept Development*, published in 1974 by IRA+ERIC/CRIER.

Making Sense demonstrates a sequential program. I hope readers will discern, as I have, the relevance of each step and find themselves wanting to help others "make sense of reading."

Helen J. James
Review Editor

Introduction

This book is intended for classroom teachers and others who are concerned and perplexed about the inability of students to understand what they read, even if they can read all the words on a printed page. The discussion is directed particularly to all classroom and reading teachers for grades six, seven, and eight.

The step-by-step approach described here was developed while trying to meet actual needs of teachers and students. Though the material is based on theory, every effort has been made to present the ideas in a practical form which is immediately applicable.

The middle grades are singled out for special attention in keeping with empirical evidence presented by Piaget and others that students, at about ages eleven to thirteen, move from a very concrete, personal view of the world toward a more abstract, objective view. This process is gradual and happens at different ages for different students. Many teachers and textbook writers assume that the process has already taken place when students move from elementary to junior high school. They take it for granted that students have received instruction and understand the grouping of ideas and their translation into paragraphs and chapters. Many students are able to find their own way, but many never grasp the basic organization of reading matter. This inability can be the result of many factors.

The basic premise of this book is that the grouping of ideas and experiences must be understood if efficient reading is to take place. Bruner and others have written about the central role of categorizing in the learning process. Grouping experience is an unconscious way of ordering impressions for survival, efficiency, and prediction for everybody; and it is also a highly sophisticated tool, consciously used in formal mental operations by some people. Each student needs to make his own tool, forged from his experiences and desires according to his native ability, with the help of teachers and models.

This book attempts to indicate possible ways of isolating, identifying, using, and integrating all of the elements necessary for understanding the basic structure of ideas. Most of the chapters deal in depth with categorizing skills, translating categories into paragraphs, or the reverse, and organizing items within paragraphs or paragraphs within larger units. This is done so that all students can understand the hierarchical organization of ideas used in reading and writing. The suggestions given are intended as takeoff points for developing understanding of more complex relationships.

The steps necessary for understanding and developing categorizing skills begin with the simplest: basic sensory experience. Evidence piles up to show that inadequate perception can so distort thinking as to make learning extremely difficult. This inadequacy can be the result of neurological or environmental factors, such as lack of communication about the environment. All sense impressions are conveyed to the brain through the nervous system. They are then sorted, some to be stored for use over a long period of time, some for temporary use, and some apparently to be discarded. The storage system used in the sorting process is crucial for remembering. An impression stored without an adequate label is hard to retrieve; it is most useful when stored under a number of different labels. Adequate storage can be done only when people are able to find common characteristics among impressions and to label them clearly. This is one of the crucial roles of language in the thinking process.

The category label, or heading, is always an abstraction, not tied to a single object, person, event, or idea. Children can visualize an elephant, a zebra, and a monkey after being introduced to them, but no one can accurately visualize the category, *Wild Animals.* On the other hand, once familiar with this label, students can easily add other animals to their list. Within the category, *Wild Animals,* they will also be able to find smaller groups, such as members of the cat family.

Problems in reading comprehension are often caused by an inability to understand the fundamental difference between general and specific ideas. Paragraphs are usually based on groups of ideas, or categories. If there is a topic sentence, it is based on the category label. Other sentences develop the specific ideas from which the label is derived. There is a profound difference between the topic sentence and other sentences, if the topic sentence is properly developed.

Visualizing objects, people, events, and relationships is essential to reading comprehension. A reader who cannot associate images with groups of words cannot understand what he reads. When subject matter at school changes from *Wild Animals* to *Parts of*

Speech or to *The Causes of the American Revolution,* students may have no way of associating these topics with any previous experience. Providing links for them is an important part of teaching.

The organization of ideas remains the same whether the subject is *Wild Animals, The Structure of the Atom,* or *Set Theory.* From the sorting of stones for tools in the Stone Age to problems of space flight, the basic pattern remains constant: Items are grouped according to a common characteristic, and this characteristic is expressed in a label or heading. If students grasp how this is done, learn to construct their own categorizing system, and use it for reading and writing, they will be better able to comprehend what they read.

This book advocates beginning every new mental task in the categorizing learning process with ideas and vocabulary already understood by all students. This is an extension of the language experience approach to reading which adds only one new learning element at a time. Students read passages they have dictated to the teacher, thereby guaranteeing familiarity with words and concepts. The only task before them is associating symbols with sounds. New thinking processes also need to be learned without unnecessary difficulties. When the process is fully understood in a familiar context, it can be applied to new ideas if the teacher provides the necessary links. Since each human being has had different experiences, several possible associations should be offered. Time must then be allowed and reinforcing activities must be undertaken in order to bring about an integration of old and new material.

Integrating many different skills is essential for reading. It has to be an extremely active process. The many symbols on a page are there in order to convey a vision from the mind of a writer to the mind of an individual reader. This form of communication is highly abstract. The reader has to work backwards from the symbols to the writer's system of ideas. First, he must translate letters into sounds, then sounds into words, and words into mental images. Beyond the letter symbols there are other symbols and visual effects which should act like traffic signals to the mind, triggering very specific mental activity. These signals include the spaces left on the page, different kinds of print, underlined portions, capitalized words, punctuation, and indentation. All of these divide the page and indicate groups of ideas. In addition, certain words and sentences should trigger an awareness of particular relationships between ideas which should help students predict what they will read next. This act of predicting and then checking the accuracy of the prediction is essential to intelligent, active reading.

Active reading means manipulation of many elements of communication. Students taught by the approach advocated in the following pages are instructed in every task expected of them, however obvious some of the tasks may appear to be. Students will proceed at different rates, but all students need to understand the process for using groups of ideas in written language in order to be able to apply the process universally. Experience in actual classroom situations shows that very competent students express appreciation for learning a system, even though their attitudes toward early steps may be condescending. Poor readers are able to learn the roles of topic and other sentences and can complete a short, formal essay. This approach has been tried in open and traditional classrooms in the seventh, eighth, and ninth grades with a variety of classroom teachers. The approach also has been used with remedial groups.

The author believes that every teacher, certainly in middle and junior high schools, should understand two aspects of reading: 1) the importance of categorizing and its role in the mental development and skill improvement of students, and 2) the visual response to the arrangement of symbols and spaces on the printed page and the way they reveal relationships.

A brief annotated bibliography appears at the end of this volume for those who are interested in the theoretical basis of the discussion and those looking for additional specific material. A glossary of key vocabulary is also provided.

No new materials are needed for implementing the type of activity advocated in this book. It is necessary, however, to use existing material in a new way.

The pronouns *he, his,* and *him* used throughout this book are intended to have a unisex meaning. Since student activities are frequently discussed, a *he/she* or *he or she* system would make for tedious reading.

CHAPTER ONE

Getting Ready

KEY VOCABULARY

category (-ies, -ize, -izing)	observe (-d, -ing, -ation)
sort (-ing)	common characteristic (-s)
group (-ing)	label (-ed, -ing)
memory (-ies, -ize, -izing)	heading
environment	efficient (-cy, -ly)
sense (-s)	problem solving
experience	predict (-ion, -ing)

KEY QUESTIONS

☐ What is categorizing and what is the role of the senses in categorizing?

☐ Why does everyone categorize?

☐ How does categorizing help people to learn and to remember?

Preview of possible answers

The environment is known only through the senses. Through the senses people are constantly bombarded with signals. The first step to good categorizing is careful observation, or good use of the senses. The signals received through the senses travel through the nervous system to the brain where they must be sorted. Exactly how this is done is not yet known, but some form of sorting has to take place or people would not be able to cope with the great number of signals. The same decisions would have to be made repeatedly. As a result of sorting experiences, habits are developed; routine ways of doing things save time and energy when they are based on careful observation.

Seeing patterns in experiences has to be learned for the sake of survival and efficiency. These patterns have to be filed in people's memories under useful headings, or labels, so they can be

1

used when needed. For example, a small child will develop a label, *Dangerous Things,* and keep adding to it: hot stoves, sharp corners, dogs, cats, electric outlets, scissors, or snatching toys from larger children. All of these different things have one common characteristic—they represent danger. The child stores the information learned from bitter experience under the label, *Dangerous Things,* in order not to repeat the same unfortunate experiences. A good filing system in the mind helps in predicting.

Introduction

Some of the elements in this chapter will be familiar and may even appear rather elementary to some teachers as well as students; and they are elementary in the same way that learning to hold the racket correctly is elementary to playing tennis. Furthermore, the author's previous attempts to teach the uses of categorizing without establishing a firm foundation revealed the necessity of the first steps.

The basic questions about categorizing must be posed first in order to tie the way humans think in real-life situations to the more abstract modes of thought needed in reading and writing. If comprehension problems are caused by lack of thinking skills, then these skills must be understood from the ground up. Students need to understand how we experience our environment and how the human mind seeks patterns even in daily experiences. These patterns, or groupings, are in fact categories; and similar categories are the foundation of formal mental operations. It is an old saying that learning takes place only when the new is tied to the familiar.

Learning to ask the right questions is often more important than finding correct answers, especially when dealing with thinking processes. Since the method advocated in this book is to first utilize and organize students' own thoughts before proceeding to new ground, questioning is especially important. It is suggested that teachers never directly formulate answers. Either a question needs to be posed in another form, or a series of questions leading up to the main one can bring responses if the first question fails. Incorrect answers are a gift since the teacher, while tactfully accepting the effort, can ask other students to comment. It is vital that a friendly, encouraging atmosphere be established in the classroom so that everybody can learn together. Taking risks has to be clearly rewarded. Organization is a very important factor in the success of any program and is especially important in this program.

It is suggested that a system be set up before activities begin. A folder for each student with a check sheet stapled inside the cover is an excellent way of keeping track of each student's work. For maximum flexibility, activities should be described only when they are undertaken. The check sheet can be divided like this:

Date	Description of the Activity	Evaluation	Comments

The evaluation may be a grade, a word, or a check mark. Space for comments is useful for requesting a rewrite or for special commendations. A time should be set aside frequently for folder review. Students need a chance to make up work missed, perhaps with the help of fellow students.

The advantages of this system are: 1) students know where they stand and can see how much they have accomplished; 2) teachers can see how each student is progressing and can produce a quick review for parents or other interested people; and 3) visitors will be impressed with the efficient organization, which will compensate for any appearance of disorder in the classroom during some activities.

The examples of activities given in this and succeeding chapters were successful with a number of students. Teachers may want to try different activities with their classes according to their special needs.

Pretesting

Those teachers who are interested in recording results of categorizing and writing activities may want to give a pretest. If students are not yet familiar with the concept of pretests, they should be advised that results will not be held against them and that pretest scores will simply be compared to scores on a similar test later which is designed to demonstrate how much has been learned at the end of a series of activities.

The first part of the pretest should consist of reading in order to identify topic sentences. The selection should have between eight and ten paragraphs, at least three of which have the topic sentence placed first and, preferably, at least one paragraph having no topic sentence. The selection should be below grade level and on an interesting topic familiar to the students. *Reader's Digest* classroom materials abound with suitable graded selections. The reading teacher should be consulted for suggestions. The reason for choosing a passage below grade level is that a thinking process is to be tested, not the ability to read words on grade level.

A statement of this nature is suitable for introducing the test:

Read the following paragraphs. When you have read the whole selection, number your sheet 1-____. Next to each number, write the first three words of the topic sentence for that paragraph. The topic sentence is the one which tells you the subject.

Evaluation should include: 1) the number of correct choices, 2) whether the correct choices were always in the initial position in the paragraph, and 3) whether the student identified the paragraphs without any topic sentence.

The second part of the pretest, given after the reading selections, should be an exercise on building a paragraph around a group of words. Four words, one of which is the label or general heading for the others, are presented with instructions as follows:

1. Write a short paragraph. Use the words listed below. Use proper paragraph form.

2. Write four short sentences, using *one* of the four words in each sentence.

3. Begin your paragraph with a *topic sentence*. One of the words gives you a *general idea*. Use that word for building your topic sentence.

The label for the three other words should be the second or third word in the list. Possible groups are:

1. English	schedule	science	math
2. electricity	oil	power	gas
3. basketball	sports	riding	tennis

Any group of words is suitable providing the subject has not been discussed in class and the concepts are familiar to every student. Evaluation is based on 1) demonstrating that paragraph form is understood; 2) using the general word for a topic sentence which accurately fits the other three words; and 3) expressing ideas clearly. In addition mechanical problems such as spelling, handwriting, or sentence structure become evident. Of the three lists of words, the third is the hardest. The topic sentence must reflect different kinds of sports: team, individual, and against an opponent.

☐ *What is categorizing and what is the role of the senses in categorizing?*

Don't emphasize the word itself, but clearly display the heading, *Category/Categorizing*, for the class. Write the word *classifying*. Everyday synonyms, like sorting or grouping, should be sought from the students. The idea of categories may be familiar to them from TV quiz shows. After preliminary, encouraging talk, three parts of the process of categorizing need to be elicited and written in correct order. This visual order is very important for future reference.

The three parts of the categorizing process which often occur almost simultaneously but which need to be understood separately for later use are: 1) sorting or grouping after careful observation, 2) recognizing the common characteristic(s), and 3) labeling accordingly.

Sorting or grouping after careful observation

Many people are not good observers and may rely too much on the sense of sight alone. To demonstrate this tendency, have the class sit still with their eyes tightly closed for at least a full minute. Then ask the group what they sensed about their environment during that minute; they will probably be astonished to discover how little they observed in the past. From *listening,* they might become aware of heating or air-conditioning, or of people breathing, fidgeting, or coughing—indicating the number of people in the room. Other sounds might reveal the kind of room or its size. From *feeling,* they might become aware of temperature; air currents; or material objects, such as clothes, chairs, desks, carpets, or floors. From *smelling,* they might discover what the home economics class is cooking or the cafeteria is preparing for lunch, whether they are indoors or out, whether someone is wearing perfume, or whether an experiment is being performed in a lab.

If the students enjoy a little drama, tell them to pretend that they have been kidnapped and blindfolded and that their survival depends on close observation. A good way to have all students participate is to have the students informally jot down what they have observed before discussing it.

Recognizing common characteristics

Show at least five objects such as a pen, pencil, eraser, sharpener, ruler, and paper. The students will quickly note that all these are writing tools, although it may take them a few moments to think of a satisfactory description. While the class is thinking of a label, the objects can be listed on the chalkboard. Suggested labels can be written on another part of the board and the students given a chance to vote on the best one and give reasons for the choice.

Labeling according to common characteristics

When the class has voted on the best label, the next question is: "Where should the label be written in relation to the list of objects?" When it has been established that the label goes above the list, the chosen label should be written there in large letters and underlined. Any objections should be fully discussed.

When the whole class is in agreement, the label should be erased and inserted in the middle of the list in place of one of the objects. The purpose of this is to get at the profound difference between the label and the objects while asking for comments on whether it belongs there. The label is not a physical object that exists but is created in the minds of people and enables them to make some sort of order out of their environment. By its very nature, the label is an abstraction, even on this level. It does not describe everything about every object but selects only that aspect which is common among all objects listed. This fact can be quickly shown by holding up only the pen, pencil, and ruler. What else do they have in common besides being writing tools? These objects are all long and narrow in shape.

The teacher should use this process of listing and labeling with other groups of objects having various commonalities. A sample group might include a duster, dish towel, sock, and tablecloth. These objects are all made of fabric, perhaps a cotton fabric, and they are flexible or soft.

Following the listing and labeling activities, the teacher should quickly review the meaning of *common characteristic*, writing the words clearly for the students. When the word, *label*, is introduced, the teacher should also write and define it for the students.

□ *Why does everyone categorize?*

This question should be preceded by others: Do all humans categorize, or group, experiences and ideas? Do primitive tribes group weather signs in order to predict the best times to plant or migrate? Do scientists group phenomena in order to establish laws of behavior? Do small children group things found to be dangerous, such as cars, electric outlets, and hot ovens? The answer, of course, is yes. It appears natural for humans to look for patterns and to name these patterns.

Why does everyone categorize? They do it for survival, efficiency, or ability to predict.

Categorizing for survival

Dogs is a good topic for stimulating discussion on this point. Many students have dogs of their own or they have learned to cope with neighborhood dogs. How do children learn to be careful with dogs? The first encounter may be with a poodle, the next with a Great Dane. How does a small child know that dogs are alike in many ways and how does a child learn that he should not take a bone away from any dog? These questions should lead to a discussion of common characteristics of dogs and provide opportunities for maximum participation by all students. Once all common characteristics are written down, the list can be labeled *Common Characteristics of Dogs*.

Another discussion topic might be *sounds*. These have much to do with survival, whether the sounds are in the jungle, on the prairie, in traffic, or in battle. A child crossing a street must be able to correctly categorize noises for survival; he must be alert enough to get out of the way of fire engines, ambulances, or police cars approaching rapidly.

Categorizing for efficiency and prediction

Students do not find it difficult to understand the need to categorize for survival, but the concepts of efficiency and prediction are considerably more difficult. Most twelve- to fifteen-year-olds have not yet experienced an urgent need for efficiency; however, it becomes important in reading and writing tasks. When efficiency is shown to mean less time spent on school work it can have considerable appeal! The same is true of the ability to predict, whether it means knowing how to please your teacher or avoiding unpleasantness.

Efficiency. This word should be interpreted as having two parts: completing tasks the quickest way and doing them the best way. Hurrying to produce a faulty product is not efficient.

To demonstrate the usefulness of categorizing, a practical task needs to be discussed. Here is one suggestion: Jack needs money. Someone in his family will help him to produce ten different designs of seasonal cards (Christmas, Easter, Valentine). Jack will post notices, tell his friends, and call his relatives. He will take orders from the samples. The orders start pouring in. What is Jack going to do with them? One person wants five of design No. 3; another wants ten of No. 7.

After posing the question, the suggestions will probably come haltingly, depending on the age of the students. The basic idea that needs to be elicited is that the only efficient way to process the orders is to categorize them. Maybe Jack can set up ten nails for the orders or clip them together by design number. Or he can enter them immediately in a book with different columns for each design number. He can then produce simultaneously the correct number of cards for each design. After the cards are produced, Jack may want to categorize them according to modes of delivery: one pile for school, one for the neighborhood, another for mailing.

Prediction. Many students are aware of predictions by Jeanne Dixon or of disasters forecast when comets visit our planet. Some may be aware that King Herod heard a prediction that a boy born in Bethlehem would become a king and that Herod consequently had all baby boys in Bethlehem killed. The students are probably much less aware of the fact that they base much of their behavior on predicting from experience.

A good discussion topic for students who have recently moved from an elementary school to a larger middle or junior high school can be how they learned to cope. How do different teachers manage their classrooms? How do students remember which books to get out of their lockers or remember homework, notes from home, money for fees, or games? Who runs around with whom? Who is a bully? Are there certain patterns of behavior which can be recognized and used to prevent making mistakes? Do students develop routines in order to stay out of trouble? These routines or habits grow out of a need to avoid making the same decisions repeatedly or encountering difficult situations.

Advantages and disadvantages of lying in bed an additional ten minutes can be considered as an example of predicting from experience. Two categories should be written under the title, *Staying in Bed.* Under *Disadvantages* student suggestions will produce items such as missing breakfast, missing the bus, making mother angry, or annoying a teacher. Under *Advantages* will come delight in remaining comfortable a few extra minutes, perhaps even delight in causing trouble, desire for attention, or relief from responsibilities such as making the bed. From surveying the two columns, a prediction can be made: to stay in bed is great, but it will cause trouble.

At school, other categories are formed: *actions that please Ms. X* or *actions that displease Mr. Y.* On the basis of these categories, a student can predict what will happen in a certain situation; and success at school is quite dependent on this ability.

□ *How does categorizing help people
to learn and to remember?*

The answer to this question will also have much to do with efficiency and prediction. The heart of the matter is that isolated items will usually be remembered for only a very short time, possibly until the next test. When items are grouped and labeled it is possible to retain them for longer periods and to reproduce them when needed.

A full file drawer can become a good analogy for students in a classroom demonstration. Ask a student to write a word on a standard sheet of paper similar to papers in the file. Ask him to place his sheet at random anywhere in the file so that no corner protrudes. Now call for a volunteer to look for the paper; his method probably will be to look at every sheet of paper in the file until he finds the proper one. Now, repeat the filing process, identifying the paper as belonging to one of the categories in the file. Have one student place the paper in that section of the file and instruct a volunteer about the file label; he then should be able to find the paper quickly and easily.

The memory of a person is similar to a file drawer, with categories developed individually according to experience. If we do not file items in our memories under a heading or label, we cannot easily find them again, if at all. Only the student knows what is already in his memory. A teacher can suggest ways to file new information (relate it to something already known), but the student must do the filing. It involves making a *decision* which only the student can make. His categories then allow information to be used again.

A demonstration of categorizing to learn and remember should include every student. Full participation is more likely to happen if each student writes suggestions before the discussion begins. Ten minutes should be ample time for informal jottings. The collected papers can provide an opportunity for evaluating thinking processes of individual students.

A problem which would provide scope might involve a student who wins a free trip to an exotic place such as India or Africa. The catch is that the winner must give a descriptive presentation to his fellow students upon his return. How will he do this? Will he have to do something during his trip to prepare for his presentation? What will he need to do?

Students could list many ways to collect and present data about the trip: observing carefully, using all senses; keeping records through written notes, tape recordings, or photographs; doing research and asking many questions; organizing information and impressions gathered from day to day; and connecting, or associating, unfamiliar things with things already known. Students may further suggest using elaborate file card systems which readily lend themselves to categorizing.

A baobab or banyan tree can serve as an example in explaining the association of new sights with familiar sights. A picture or sketch of the tree can be shown to the students. Suppose that the camera was out of film the day the traveler saw the tree. How will it be described? Someone in the class may suggest talking about common characteristics of trees. This situation provides an opportunity to show how people can compare and contrast items within a known category in order to include new items. Oaks, maples, and pines are known by sight. Banyan or baobab trees, although strange looking to some, share a sufficient number of characteristics with known trees to enable them to be categorized as trees.

The winning student's final presentation might be organized around chosen categories such as amusing incidents, geographic features, climate, vegetation, local customs, food, language, dress, and history. The student will not be able to include all of his experiences in a brief talk and, therefore, will have to be *selective* about examples. He will have to remember that his listeners will not have had the same experiences that he has had and that he must be careful not to take too much for granted.

This class discussion could be followed by two-minute individual student presentations of one limited category from the curriculum or the environment. This activity would involve reading for a narrow purpose and selecting only relevant material. The main focus in the presentation should be a clear description of the common characteristic(s) of a particular category.

In these activities, it would be wise not to force presentations which are too advanced. The goal is to help students understand the uses of categorizing in learning. The thought processes are more significant than the number of visual aids produced. Students who think things through carefully should be rewarded even if their presentations are not elegant. Handicapped readers and writers need every encouragement at this stage.

Another good exercise for showing the value of categorizing involves the memorizing of syllables. Each student should first be given ten unordered nonsense syllables. A sample list follows:

Nonsense Syllables

sib	har
mel	wix
fap	zok
vot	jod
ceg	bef

The students should study the list for two minutes and then write down as many syllables as they can remember. After completing this exercise, a new carefully alphabetized list should be treated the same way. A sample list follows:

Nonsense Syllables in Alphabetical Order

baz	har
cex	jep
div	kig
fot	lom
gus	mul

If all goes well, the class will do much better on the second list, since only the last letter of each syllable has to be memorized. Note that the words are arranged in alphabetical order and that the medial vowels in each column are in regular vowel order of *a, e, i, o, u.*

It would then be valuable to have students try individually to order the first list to see whether patterns exist. Two possibilities are obvious: straight alphabetizing and ordering alphabetically according to the medial vowels. Samples follow:

bef		fap	jod
ceg	two *e*'s	har	vot
fap			zok
har	two *a*'s	bef	
jod		ceg	
mel		mel	
sib		sib	no syllables
vot	alternating	wix	with *u*
wix	*i* and *o*		
zok			

Many spelling and vocabulary lists given to students with inadequate discussion mean no more to them than the sample list of nonsense syllables. Consequently, students can neither understand nor remember the words. The lists need to be organized into spelling patterns and meaning categories.

Conclusion

The activities in this chapter should help students to understand what categories are and why we need and use them. The important role of the senses and of careful observation needs to be stressed. Without careful observation, people categorize incorrectly and, therefore, predict and decide inadequately.

Evaluation

The purpose of evaluation is to allow students and teachers to become aware of how much the students have really understood. Most students, having participated in these activities, should discover that they have understood.

A careful oral review of the key vocabulary words is essential before evaluation (see the glossary). Neither the words nor the concepts are easy. After the review, it is necessary to make certain that every student can recognize and understand the vocabulary. Usage during later work should help to teach spelling, which is less important than understanding at this stage.

One way of reviewing is to ask whether groups of words can be formed under labels. Examples follow:

Benefits of Categorizing
efficiency
memorizing
predicting
problem solving
habits

Process (Way) of Categorizing
sorting
grouping
categorizing
common characteristic
labeling

What People Use for Categorizing
senses
environment
experience
observation

Grouping the words provides an easy form of individual evaluation. The words should be presented in the original order without labels. Students can then fill in words under different labels.

Examples: *Words Which Tell About Ways Grouping Things Helps Us, Words Describing the Way Things Are Grouped,* and *Words Connected with What We Need for Sorting.*

Even though spelling is not an immediate goal, students should be encouraged to copy words correctly and should be required to rewrite misspelled words correctly to erase any words learned incorrectly. Correct copying should be stressed throughout all of the activities described in these chapters. Students who consistently copy incorrectly need special help. Phonic patterns may need to be reviewed; on the other hand, students may be seeing distortions rather than being careless.

Another way of evaluating understanding is to present two vocabulary words in an incomplete sentence and ask for completion.

EXAMPLES

- *Sorting* or *grouping* can also be called (categorizing)
- We *observe* with our *senses* and this leads to finding (either categories or common characteristics)
- A *category label* or *heading* is based on (a common characteristic)
- *Predicting* and *problem solving* are greatly improved through careful (categorizing)
- *Memorizing* is helped greatly by filing *experiences* under good (labels or categories)

Teachers may want to use a reading passage as another means of evaluation. Following are two paragraphs and a few comprehension questions. The paragraphs should be read aloud while students follow the text on an overhead or individual sheet.

1. Everyone makes categories, or groups, from experiences in three steps: by observing with the senses, by deciding what certain experiences have in common, and by making a label with the common characteristic.
2. Categories help to make order out of the many events people experience. This order improves the way events are understood and remembered. It also improves prediction, problem solving, and efficiency.

Questions

1. Which paragraph tells you why categories help people?
   1. _____
   2. _____
      (2 is correct)

2. Categories are made from:
   a. predictions
   b. characteristics
   c. labels
   d. experiences
   (d is correct)
3. The first step in categorizing is:
   a. efficiency
   b. finding what things have in common
   c. observing with the senses
   d. labeling
   (c is correct)
4. Which of the following statements are about ways categorizing helps people to think better?
   a. categorizing experiences helps to make order out of them
   b. categorizing helps people to predict
   c. categorizing helps people to see better
   d. categorizing experiences makes them easier to remember
   (a, b, and d are correct)
5. The category labels are made from:
   a. experiences
   b. common characteristics
   c. senses
   d. problems
   (b is correct)

This evaluation is, in itself, a review, but it will show the teacher which students need further help. Any of the above questions answered incorrectly indicate an immediate need for further training, perhaps by peer teachers who have shown a clear grasp of the material. The students who need review also need another opportunity to complete the evaluation for a satisfactory grade. No student should experience failure since successful completion of each step is necessary before going on to the next step. A free reading period or other activity for those who complete everything quickly can become a practical solution to the different rates of learning.

CHAPTER TWO

Some Different Ways of Categorizing

KEY VOCABULARY

relationship	item (-s)
form	label
function	title
texture	language
material	communicate (-tion)
flexible	

KEY QUESTIONS

☐ Can an object be categorized in different ways?

☐ Is there a need to observe carefully to categorize well?

☐ What are some ways in which one can categorize?

☐ Is there a difference between form and function?

☐ Can the same object perform different functions?

☐ Is it important to know many different ways of categorizing for solving problems?

Preview of Possible Answers

Physical objects can be categorized in many different ways according to the need of the moment. Words can also be categorized in various ways.

Whether working with objects or words, people must observe carefully in order to categorize well. Then, language is needed to describe what has been observed. An accurate label for a category will make it easier to share thoughts and communicate with other people.

The form of an object, which remains essentially the same, may be the basis of categorizing. On the other hand, the basis may be the different functions of an object. The ability to be flexible and to categorize in different ways is important in problem solving.

Introduction

Classroom teachers may feel that the questions to be asked and answered in this chapter are unrelated to the immediate tasks, reading and writing. The questions are, however, absolutely basic to the understanding of the organization of ideas. It is precisely the lack of insight into these basic thought processes that leads to poor reading comprehension and the inability to organize ideas in writing. If students see only isolated ideas of the same value when they read, they can never hope to grasp the relationship between superordinate main ideas and subordinate specific items. An inability to retain what is read will naturally follow this lack of grouping and labeling.

Equally important is the concept that categorizing an object, a word, or a fact in one way by no means describes it. The object has been related to other objects in one way only and may be related to other objects in other ways. Full description occurs only when all possible ways of categorizing have been exhausted. Seeing an object, a word, or a fact in only one way brings on mental rigidity and inhibits the ability to do problem solving.

It is often said that education consists of learning to ask the right questions. The activities in this chapter are designed to help students ask some very basic questions about relationships.

□ *Can an object be categorized in different ways?*

A good introduction to answering this question is to show an actual object. Can this object be categorized (described) in different ways? An object such as a student notebook offers good possibilities. As students respond with suggestions, other objects in the room should be sought which are also related to the notebook in that special way. For instance, if a student suggests *color* and the notebook is blue, other blue objects in the room can be listed along with the notebook under the label *Blue Objects in the Classroom*. It is essential to label each group and this task can be accomplished by different students. Eventually, the labels may include *Objects that Hold Written Work* (function), *Cotton and Cardboard Objects* (material), *Rectangular Objects* (shape), *Objects Approximately 9" by 12"* (size), and *Objects in Worn Condition* (age or condition).

At first students may not offer exact terminology. Meaningful words can be accepted while pressing for more accurate descriptions. References to science and math may be helpful, since the students may know terms from these subjects and not realize their application. Precise terminology eventually becomes important because students will encounter these words in their reading. They do not read, "What the Supreme Court is there to do is . . . ." They read, "The function of the Supreme Court is . . . ."

□ *Is there a need to observe carefully in order to categorize well?*

During the discussion about different ways to categorize an object, a number of inaccurate responses will probably stem from poor observation. Such responses can be capitalized upon. If no mistakes are made, an object can be passed around for handling in order to describe its texture. Scraps of fabric, which look soft and smooth but feel rough or scratchy, are excellent for this activity.

This question is referred to again in Chapter 3 with the query, "What are some of the dangers of categorizing?" If a student mentions problems of prejudice here, the discussion should deal with the question at this point rather than later.

□ *What are some ways in which one can categorize?*

A review of different ways of categorizing and listing will reinforce learning at this point, even though the topics were covered while categorizing the notebook (or other object). Students may wish to add other ways related to science, such as mass or area. It may be desirable to wander further afield and talk about the use of the various senses in categorizing. For instance, hearing will bring in a new dimension—the categorizing of sounds. For example, do tennis players rely heavily on the sound of the ball as it leaves the opponent's racket? Do they categorize the sounds and then predict where the ball will go? Do experienced drivers check the sounds of their cars or motorbikes for possible trouble? If somebody hears a scary noise at night, does that person listen intently to identify the sound, then categorize it as dangerous or as a normal domestic or neighborhood sound? Hunting is another good topic for illustrating the use of senses for categorizing and then predicting.

There may be good reasons for making a list of many ways to categorize; or the class may be content with learning a few important ways, depending largely on the students and the special interests of the teacher. However, do not bore students with prolonged discussion.

☐ *Is there a difference between form and function?*
☐ *Can the same object perform different functions?*

The first of these two questions should be explained in terms of the second. By discussing the different functions of an object, students can see that form is largely static whereas functions change according to need.

Many students have difficulty understanding the difference between form and function. This difference becomes important in developing ability to categorize flexibly, to see connections between apparently different items, and to select accurate language. The student who has a problem with this distinction typically sees form and function as the same, usually directly related to personal experience. "A spoon is for eating my cereal."

A tablespoon can become an appropriate object for demonstrating the difference between form and function. After considering the spoon and the components of its form—handle and shallow bowl—a chalkboard heading of *Tablespoon* can be written above two columns; *Form* on the left and *Function* on the right. Under *Form*, the only item will be a drawing of the spoon in the middle of the column. Students can then contribute possible functions of the spoon to be listed in the right column, such as eating, stirring, serving, digging, removing lids, drumming, and attacking with sharpened handle.

A variety of spoons (the school cafeteria is a good source) can be used to demonstrate a more complex relationship of form to function. Are there elements of form shared by all the spoons? Yes, the handle and bowl are common to all objects called spoons. A new listing on the chalkboard, *Various Spoons,* can include the divisions of *Form* and *Function.* Under *Form,* this time it will be necessary to write a description of each spoon, including always the handle and bowl common to all. For example, a large spoon for stirring would be described: handle—1 foot long; bowl—5 inches, shallow. The words *for stirring* would go on the function side. Why is this spoon not appropriate for serving or eating? What aspects of the form give it a specialized function? Are other functions possible, such as propping up a window? The discussion should encourage students to analyze both form and function of objects.

Another object should be chosen for quick application of concepts learned during the previous discussion. A cowboy hat has some appeal and all students have seen Westerns on TV. A student-led discussion on the specific hat should lead to exploration of other hats. It is necessary to remember the importance of the titles on the chalkboard: first *Cowboy Hat,* then *Various Hats* or something similar. Acting out roles for the different hats can be a vivid way of expressing function.

A more difficult, but very important, area for analyzing form and function is language. Once again, a specific word is the best introduction. The word *h i t* is useful and liked by the students. This word becomes the title, in the same way that *Tablespoon* and *Cowboy Hat* were the titles for specific objects. (A teacher will have to decide whether to also use the word with a capital *H.* The word *H i t* can be written as a separate title halfway down the board or else dealt with afterwards.) The form of the word consists of three letters (*h i t*) of the alphabet *in that order* (conceivably words like *t i h* or *i t h* might exist). These letters will be written in the *Form* column. If all the students are well grounded in grammar, it might be feasible to label the functions of the word. It is probably more useful to give examples and describe in other terms what the word *does* in the sentence. Some examples of *h i t* functions are these: hit the ball (doing word), the second hit of the baseball game (event), the show was a hit (description of success), the gang planned a hit on the bank (robbery), that hits the spot (an application of a remedy), Huck Finn hit the road (he left), she hit on an idea (it came to her), Mary and Jack hit if off well (they got along). The functions of *h i t* would probably be confined to the imperative use of the word at the beginning of a sentence. This limited meaning of the word would be used to describe various acts of hitting, as with the hand or a weapon.

The procedure used with *h i t* should lead to another student-led discussion of a similar word. *G o* is a good possibility: did go; will go; had a go; Oh, go away!; he's very go-ahead; getting the go-ahead sign; Oh, go on!; Don't go!; go along with something. Understanding the different functions of the word is most important. Even though these functions do not receive grammatical labels, they can contribute to the general description of the word.

After defining *h i t* and another word by form and function, a listing of *Various Words* can follow, paralleling the listings of *Various Spoons* and *Various Hats.* Once again, the basic form of a word must be sought—the root word. Just as there are variations on the basic forms of spoons and hats, so there are variations on root words. The reason for the variations is *need.*

The words chosen at this point might well be the ones learned in these first two chapters, starting with *category* itself. A listing might look something like this:

Various Words

Form	Function
category	A grouping and labeling of items (noun)
categories	More than one of the above (plural noun)
categorize	The act of grouping and labeling (verb—present, future, one or more people)
categorized	The act done usually in the past (verb)
categorizing	The name of the act (noun) or the act itself showing more complex time relationships (he was categorizing, they will be categorizing)

Since its derivatives follow a similar pattern, *memory* might be a good second word. *Observe, label, predict, relate, form,* and *function* would all be suitable words. Again, the object of this activity is not to concentrate on the grammatical labels but to understand why we need to vary form for different functions and exactly what these different functions are. If the discussion remains in this channel, the students will, hopefully, realize that each small variation of form—the adding of an *s* or *d*—is significant in terms of function. Are these variations printed on the page to thwart and frustrate us in our reading? On the contrary, they are there in order to clarify the exact function of the word. A few mistaken uses of form will perhaps demonstrate this:

> She was category the objects. (categorizing)
> He had wonderful memory of the trip. (memories, or a wonderful memory)
> The observe in the lab proved the theory of gravity. (observation)
> George was busy label the cans. (labeling)
> Jeanne Dixon's predict was that it would rain. (prediction)
> The relate between form and function is important. (relationship)
> The coach was form the team for the season. (forming)
> The computer was not function for the election. (functioning)

From this discussion, the realization may follow that there are categories of words, just as there are categories of objects or sounds. Certain standard variations help in simplifying categorization of words and aid students in accurately understanding what the words are doing in a sentence.

A new listing can be made to demonstrate this principle, granting at the outset that the English language is not as tidy about variations as are many other languages. Students learning another language may contribute examples of standard variations in that language. The new listing need not be exhaustive; for example:

STANDARD VARIATIONS OF WORDS TO SHOW FUNCTION

Root Word (Noun)	Noun Plural	Basic Verb	Past Tense
category	categories	categorize	categorized
memory	memories	memorize	memorized
monopoly	monopolies	monopolize	monopolized
form	forms	form	formed
label	labels	label	labeled
review	reviews	review	reviewed

Categorizing of words could go on forever and, indeed, could be a useful way of reviewing basic forms throughout the school year. At the moment however, it is essential to limit the process to the relationship between form and function. Prefixes and suffixes would be an appropriate subject for a brief discussion since the presence of one of these as part of a word *form* determines (or reveals) the word's *function* in a sentence. The discussion should not be prolonged beyond class interest.

Whether reading, talking, or writing about objects or words, students can be taught to observe and analyze both form and function. Are there questions students can learn to ask? The basic question about form concerns how a person perceives the object or word through the senses—the only way external things can be perceived. How does it look, feel, taste, sound, and smell? The basic question can lead to subdivisions (color, shape, size, material and condition) preceded by the word *what*: What color is it? The basic question for function is very simple: What does it do? Although there is only one part to the question, the answers may be numerous.

Form remains essentially unchanged and, therefore, recognizable; whereas, function varies according to need. When students accept that reality, they gain a foundation for finer details of categorization.

□ *Is it important to know many different*
ways of categorizing for solving problems?

This question has been answered partially in the preceding discussions, but formal review and clarification are necessary. Vivid presentations can be developed through the use of famous prisoner-of-war escapes, well known crimes, or dramatic rescues. Students may give examples from books they have read or from movies and television programs. Many of the escapades on *Mission Impossible* provide novel ways of categorizing objects or events. Disguise is essentially a way of changing form and using that form to perform functions not normally associated with it. In one famous prison break of German internees in India during World War II, the men marched out the front gate in drill formation, disguised in British uniforms, relying on the guard's interpretation of this movement as legitimate because of the uniforms.

Students should provide other instances from science and technology where a discovery hinged on the ability to categorize something in a new way. We would never have known the benefits of penicillin had Sir Alexander Fleming thought of mold as performing a limited function only. After this type of discovery people often say, "But it was so simple!" It resulted from an ability to shift things from traditional categories to new categories.

Writers have problems attracting the attention of their readers; therefore, they create new ways of looking at a subject. Sports writers look for unusual qualities or experiences in a player. An article may have a paragraph portraying a sports hero as an excellent student. This category may include grades, honors, and degrees obtained.

In math, we learn in a variety of ways to group numbers for faster and more accurate calculations. There are ways of checking operations which regroup the numbers of the original problem. Algebraic equations can be simplified according to laws of regrouping. Multiplication must have originally developed as a quick way to do addition because someone became tired of adding six bushels of grain over and over again and developed a systematic way of grouping numbers—the result being the multiplication tables.

Conclusion

The ability to categorize in different ways is an essential part of solving problems and meeting needs, regardless of the nature of the problem. All subject matter in schools offers opportunities for practice.

Evaluation

This evaluation may depend, in part, on the extent of student participation in the previous activities. If the teacher has had a chance to observe each student in action, the evaluation can be very brief. If a few vocal students have dominated the scene, a more extensive evaluation will be necessary. The more vocal students could receive another assignment, be excused, or be asked to work out an evaluation for the group.

The vocabulary words at the beginning of the chapter should be reviewed. The word *label* can here be defined as the heading of one single category, whereas the word *title* would be a heading for more than one category. (Later chapters will deal extensively with these words.) The extent of the discussion of the word *language* will depend on the curriculum. While there are other "languages" (body language, animal signals), the use of *language* here is limited to communication among people through systematic use of words.

After reviewing the vocabulary with the words displayed, the students may answer a few questions.

Examples

1. An object can have one (form) but many (function) s.

2. A basic *form* can be varied to fill a need and perform a special (function) .

3. We may be able to form categories in our minds without language, but we usually need language to (communicate) our ideas to other people.

4. What *kind* of relationship do the following items have?

    car/bicycle/baby carriage (wheeled vehicles)
                               (perform similar functions)

5. Can the name of this relationship become a category *label* for those objects? No ____ Yes (√)

6. Determine which of the listed relationships these words have:

    spoon
    cowboy hat
    hit
    go

    a. they are all the same size
    b. they are all concrete objects
    c. they have one simple form but many different functions

    (*c* is correct)

7. If a ruler is categorized as a *Measuring Instrument,* is it fully described? Yes ____ No (√)

8. If your answer on 7 was *no,* write two other ways to describe the item. (hard)   (long, thin rectangle)

9. Make a category out of these four words:

ice cream   cakes   desserts   pies

Label _____   _____

_____   _____

(*desserts* is the label)

10. When you have a problem to solve you must be __(flexible)__ about the way you categorize.

A reading passage with comprehension questions again may be helpful. The best method is to read the text aloud while students follow. Thinking is to be evaluated rather than ability to read the words.

1. There are many different ways of categorizing. Among these, form and function are important. Being flexible enough to see that one object can be grouped with many different kinds of objects is also important.

2. Objects, words, ideas, or people can be grouped by identifying what they have in common or stating their relationship. This relationship is indicated in a category by the label. Many different categories can be gathered under one title. The title also states what the categories have in common.

3. People can see and think about categories without always using language, but language is needed for talking to other people. Carefully choosing words enables one to communicate more easily.

Questions

1. Which paragraph says that the word *relationship* means having something in common? 1. ____ 2. (✓) 3. ____

2. Flexibility and ability to find different ways of relating one object to other objects are important. True (✓) False ____

3. A title is like a label for a number of different categories. True (✓) False ____

4. Language is:
   a. made up of words
   b. useful for communicating about categories
   c. necessary for seeing and thinking about categories

   (*a* and *b* are correct)

5. It is easier to communicate if:
   a. language is used
   b. we talk only about categories
   c. we choose words carefully

   (*a* and *c* are correct)

CHAPTER THREE

Categorizing of Objects Leading to Sentence Writing

KEY VOCABULARY

label	paragraph
item (-s)	topic sentence
general	process
specific	product
miscellaneous	abstract (-tion, -tions)
symbol (-s)	concrete

KEY QUESTIONS

☐ Can different ways of categorizing be demonstrated with actual objects?

☐ How can categorizing lead to sentence writing?

☐ Is there a possible relationship between a category and a paragraph?

Preview of possible answers

Objects can be categorized in different ways such as function, color, texture, and form.

Similar processes are used in forming categories and paragraphs and each process involves grouping items by common characteristics. All formal categories have labels. Not all paragraphs have topic sentences, but a general label could be given which describes what the sentences have in common.

The product of categorizing is usually an abstract grouping of items in one's mind. The product of paragraph creation is a physical grouping of sentences for the benefit of a reader to enable him to better understand the relationship of ideas in written form.

Both categorizing and paragraph creation are organizational processes used to improve understanding.

Introduction

Children cannot suddenly learn abstract ways of thinking. Step-by-step progress toward abstract thinking should evolve from a variety of concrete, real-life experiences. In many homes, children learn thinking processes and related words through parent instruction about the names and uses of objects. A father may take a nail (or some harmful object) out of his child's mouth and say, "No! That is a nail, *not* food. Nails are used to join pieces of wood, like this," and he demonstrates. In this one statement, the father has revealed to the child the name of the object, its function, what it is *not,* and another item in the same category. If he also demonstrates driving a nail, he may use a hammer. The child then has a category which includes nails, wood, and hammer.

Many children are denied this kind of experience at home. Regardless of education or economic backgrounds, busy parents often do not understand the importance of *conversation.* Basic learning is best experienced in a concrete way. Children who are denied these opportunities at home especially need them at school. Working out a systematic instructional program to provide concrete experiences benefits all children. Children who have been fortunate at home can further refine their thought processes and learn creative uses of them.

Categorizing of objects in the classroom is good practice for groups of students. These objects can be physically manipulated and placed into groups. While the students must have some label, or common characteristic, in mind when they physically sort the objects, they may not normally put these thoughts into exact words. Requiring students to write category labels for the group of objects encourages thinking and development of appropriate words.

Later, if students have problems with paragraph construction and analysis (reading) or with hierarchies of ideas, a teacher and student can discuss the concrete image of categorizing objects. This concrete image then serves as a bridge to the abstract organization of ideas.

Practical suggestions

The sample list of objects which follows may guide teachers in selections of objects. For practical reasons, selected items should be small, not too fragile, varied, and yet familiar to students. To be categorized by function, color, texture, shape, or material individual objects should not represent too many categories. Care should be taken to include three of each type of object in at least four categories.

Some of the objects listed are of special value. For later use, students need to be introduced to the concept of symbols. It is, therefore, necessary to have at least three simple examples of symbols. A letter and a number should be included in forms that are usable for ways of categorizing other than by function. The birthday candle in the shape of a number is especially useful. A miniature flag, traffic signal, valentine heart, or similar object could round out the category and provide different types of symbols.

STUDENT DESCRIPTION OF OBJECTS

	Function	Color (predominant)	Texture
paper cup	container, birthday decoration	green	smooth
birthday candle (in the shape of number 6)	decoration, symbol, power source	blue	smooth and waxy
battery	power source	silver	smooth
fuse	part of power system	gold	grooved edge, smooth top and bottom
drapery hook	connector, decoration aid	silver	smooth, with sharp end
key ring	connector	silver	smooth, sharp catch
hook (clothing)	connector	silver	smooth, sharp ends
make-up brush	cosmetic aid	red and black	smooth handle, soft brush
powder puff	cosmetic utensil	blue	soft
mascara tube	cosmetic decoration	any color	smooth, rough top, sharp ends
folded rain cap in case	protection, decorative clothing	red	smooth, waxy
pencil	writing tool	yellow	smooth, sharp point, spongy eraser
ruler	writing and measuring tool	clear, black lines	smooth with ridges
notebook (pocket)	writing material (decorative)	yellow	smooth, waxy, sharp spiral end
pencil sharpener (pocket)	tool for repairing writing instruments	red	ridged, sharp blade
protractor	measuring tool	clear, black lines	smooth with ridges
rubber band	connector, weapon	yellow	sticky, spongy
cloth leaf	decoration	green	smooth one side, scratchy other
letter M (felt)	decoration, symbol	green	soft
tanned leather	protection (coats), clothing material	black	smooth one side, sticky other
picture hook (cloth-backed)	decoration, connector	silver, white	smooth hook, scratchy backing
yarn	clothing material	red	soft
eraser	writing tool accessory	yellow	spongy
button	connector, decoration, clothing	green	smooth
diaper pin	connector, clothing	silver and blue	smooth, sharp point
fabric scrap	clothing material, decoration	green	smooth one side, scratchy other
miniature flag	symbol, decoration	red, white, and blue	smooth

A group of four or five pupils appears to be the optimum size for categorizing objects. A group of this number encourages individual participation and provides for different points of view as well. Care should be given to the grouping; and each group should include at least one articulate, interested student and at least one other student whose strengths are in writing and spelling.

The duration of the activities will depend on the kinds of students in the class, the teacher's interests, and the number of fringe benefits desired. (Vocabulary concepts, precision of language, the clarification and justification of thought processes, and spelling can all be included formally or informally.) Categorizing the objects at least three times in three different ways is necessary. Each way can be done in one class period of forty minutes if there are enough sets of objects for the whole class.

Before the first session, care should be taken to explain the purpose of the activity and to discuss physical arrangements such as furniture moving and grouping. This is in itself an exercise in problem solving, organizational skills, and efficiency. Some classes enjoy racing the clock to see how quickly they can get ready; time can then be improved by discussing trouble areas at the next session. Trouble areas can be labeled: *Moving of Furniture, Moving of People,* and *Noise.* It is important to allow enough time at the end of the session for putting everything away—probably five minutes is needed when only the objects have to be put away.

REQUIREMENTS FOR EACH GROUP

1. A central, flat area about 3' x 3' (for spreading out objects) plus ample surrounding space for four or five students.
2. A box or bag containing
   - 20 or more objects
   - 20 or more pieces of cardboard about 3" x 4" (for writing labels)
   - 5 or more pieces of cardboard about 5" x 7" (for writing titles)
   - Rubber bands (for collecting sets of labels and titles after each session)
   - A different colored felt-tipped pen for each group of students (for identifying work done by each group). *The writing on titles and labels should be large and legible.*

□ *Can different ways of categorizing be
demonstrated with actual objects?*

The group activity can now begin with clear, concise instructions. Students sort the objects into groups having common characteristics. (Different ways of categorizing should not be reviewed at this point as the whole exercise is designed to help students see problems for themselves and find their own solutions.) When all students in a group agree about the sorting, they should write a label clearly for each set of objects; then, one student should write a title for all of the objects and all of the labels.

It is very important for the teacher to circulate constantly during the categorizing to observe problems that arise and to note how they are solved. Frustrations should not be allowed to take over, but the teacher should never contribute the whole solution. If mistakes are made and not corrected by the time the title is written, other students should be asked to find the error and explain the reasons for the error. Was poor categorizing due to poor observation, inconsistent categorizing, or inexact choice of words?

Some predictable problem questions may arise. If objects have more than one color, texture, or material, how are they to be labeled? There can be a category called *Multicolored Objects* or *Objects Made of Two or More Materials*. If students categorize groups of objects in more than one way, what will happen? They will have to regroup to write the title unless the title includes the different ways they are categorized; even so, their title will be incorrect unless they use the word *or* between the kinds of categories (*Objects Categorized by Function or Color*). If they write the word *and* , it will not fit since all the objects have not been categorized both ways. How will the students know what to use for the title? Ask them *how* they categorized and *what* they categorized. The answers will become the two parts of the title (*A Collection of Objects Categorized by Color* or *School and Household Objects* or *Miscellaneous Objects Categorized by Color*).

When all the groups have finished, one student from each group can move to another group for five minutes to see what was done and to find possible mistakes. The students can then read and compare titles and labels for whole class discussion. Possible topics could center around the language chosen, suitability of titles and labels, consistency of categorizing, and the number of categories. Many different approaches are possible, all of which could be right in terms of inner logic.

At the conclusion of the activity, pupils for each group should return all objects, bundled title and labels, extras, and the felt-tip pen to the bag or box. This container is then identified by the color of the pen.

It is possible that different cultures have different ways of initial categorizing. This writer found that in one school system on three grade levels all the students who worked on categorizing objects initially categorized by function. There were no exceptions even though categorizing by color would have been far simpler. If a whole class or group of students does categorize by function, then all can afterwards proceed with another method chosen by the teacher. Should some groups initially categorize by color, or by some method other than function, the program will have to be adjusted accordingly.

The second categorizing should take place within a few days of the first. This activity may go twice as fast as the initial one, and there may be ample time for class discussion. A valuable procedure is to "follow" one or two objects and see how they are grouped in the two sessions. Two important questions will be: Did you have to change the labels? Did you have to change the title? Any regrouping of the objects, of course, necessitates changing labels; when these are changed, the title must change too. If the birthday candle is changed from a *decoration* or *power source* to a *blue object,* the title must change from *Objects Categorized by Function* to *Objects Categorized by Color.*

A few days later, the students should categorize by a third method. (More methods can be used if the teacher feels that the students need them.) When the last categorizing has been completed, the students should arrange everything in a hierarchy: title in the center of the work space at one end, labels in a row below the title, and objects below each appropriate label. This hierarchical arrangement will be referred to later during reading and writing activities.

□ *How can categorizing lead to sentence writing?*

The answer to this question is the writing of topic sentences to go with each label and set of objects. Each student should write the sentences while looking at the labels and objects. A good bridge to this new activity can be provided through the duplicated worksheet (see sample). Each student should receive a worksheet, but the sentences probably will evolve from group discussion.

When all students have completed at least one topic sentence, one group can write an example on the chalkboard. This example should include the title of the whole collection, one label and a list of three objects, and a topic sentence next to the label. Once this model has been seen and approved, other students can provide additional oral or written responses. If the "formula" suggested is not used, but the sentence is appropriate, the student volunteering should of course not be penalized. At this point, the objective is to show that the label is used for the creation of the topic sentence rather than to produce beautiful sentences. Chapter 5 provides further opportunities for practice.

Ten minutes should be allowed at the end of this session for a final look at the hierarchy of title, labels, and objects; and each student should describe it on paper as illustrated in the following sample, with categories listed one under another. This is the way the hierarchy would appear if translated into paragraphs in a text:

TITLE

Label 1
Three objects

Label 2
Three objects
etc.

(Sample worksheet)   Student name _____
                                  Class _____

WRITING TOPIC SENTENCES FROM LABELS

Directions.   Choose three labels and groups of objects from those in front of you. Write the labels on the lines provided. Below the label, list three to five objects in the group. Above these copy the title you have chosen for this way of categorizing the groups.

Next to each label write a topic sentence. This is a general sentence often used in a paragraph to tell the reader the main idea of the paragraph. The sentence must fit *all* the objects and the title, and it must use the label. An easy way to start the sentence is: "There are some (or a few, many, several, three) __(label)__ objects . . ." and round out the sentence with ". . . in this collection" or a similar phrase. DO NOT MENTION ANY OF THE OBJECTS IN THIS GENERAL SENTENCE.

(Title) _____

1. *Label*   _____   Topic Sentence   _____
   Objects   _____   _____
               _____
               _____
               _____
               _____

2. *Label* _____ Topic Sentence _____
   Objects _____   _____
            _____
            _____
            _____
            _____

3. *Label* _____ Topic Sentence _____
   Objects _____   _____
            _____
            _____
            _____
            _____

The teacher might write an example like this on the chalkboard:

Miscellaneous Objects Categorized by Function

Label	Objects used as symbols	*Topic Sentence*	There are some
Objects	letter M		objects in this collection that
	candle (shape of 6)		are used as symbols.
	miniature flag		

☐ *Is there a possible relationship*
  between a category and a paragraph?

This question has been answered in part by the writing of topic sentences based on the category labels. A formal, comparative approach will reveal other similarities. Before starting this discussion, each student should read a very brief paragraph, preferably in printed material, about something every student understands. One student can read it aloud. The paragraph chosen must have the topic sentence at the beginning. (If a student points out that these sentences also appear in the middle or at the end, he should be congratulated. The teacher can explain that, at the moment, the simplest type of paragraph structure will be used.) This sentence should be identified and a student asked to translate it into a simple label, which can be written on the chalkboard. Simple phrases representing the sense of the other sentences can then be written under this label. For example:

Label	**Beautiful Day**	**It was a beautiful day.**
Items	sun shining	The sun was shining. Little
	blue sky with clouds	clouds raced across the blue
	breeze	sky. A gentle breeze kept
		the warm air fresh.

The comparison between paragraphs and categories should include both the *process* of creation and the *product* (these can be translated as *"the way* it is formed" and *"what* is formed"). This distinction is important as the process is the same, even though the product may look very different. (An analogy might be the comparison of a quick sketch for a painting with the final painting itself. The sketch contains the essential elements but not the color and detail.) After the discussion, something like this might be put on the chalkboard:

COMPARISON OF CATEGORIES AND PARAGRAPHS

Categories	Paragraphs
Process for making categories	*Process* for making paragraphs
• Sorting or grouping items	• Sorting or grouping ideas
• Labeling the items according to common characteristic	• Making a general statement about these ideas
Product	*Product*
• Label—general statement based on common characteristic (never one object or item)	• Topic sentence—general statement based on the common aspect of the ideas
• Items—specific objects, ideas, sounds, events, words	• Other sentences—based on specific ideas, examples, reasons

If the distinction between process and product is still not clear to students, examples from daily life can be helpful. The *process* of cooking a meal can be analyzed as 1) collecting raw materials, taking food out of the freezer, checking leftovers, and 2) providing heat for cooking (formerly a complex part of the process when wood had to be chopped or coal hauled). The *product,* then, is the meal on the table. Other examples can come from shop, home economics, and manufacturing.

Conclusion

Before reviewing all vocabulary words, it is often wise to devote extra time to the words *general* and *specific* and their relationship to each other. One way to do this is to ask the students, "What did you find when you sat down to categorize the objects?" The answer should be that there were objects and blank cardboard rectangles. If someone says that there were *labels,* the student must immediately receive the correct information that there were only blank pieces of cardboard. Why were words written later on this cardboard? Did the words say something about the objects? Were any labels the same as any *one* object? Why not? Did any label completely describe any one object?

A category label always makes a general statement about a group of specific items (the word *item* is used to get around listing objects, ideas, words, people, numbers, and phenomena). The item may be abstract in nature, such as *love, beliefs, numbers,* or *space.* Even large abstractions are subordinate to the general label. This label can be translated into a general statement, or topic sentence. The labels, in turn, are subordinate to the title. Since the topic will be discussed in Chapter 4, only the relationship between general and specific statements is mentioned here.

In summary, category labels are abstractions of the human mind, even when they are words written on paper or cardboard. These labels are not like other objects, nor do they describe everything about a particular object. For example, categorizing the blue, wax, birthday candle in the shape of a six as a *symbol* tells us only one thing: the candle is made in the shape of a number. Placed with *fuse* and *battery* and labeled *Sources of Power,* the item is described only as a source of light and heat. Each label for the candle focuses on only one quality of the candle which makes it belong with other things. Often these other objects do not look at all like the candle. Labels are by their very nature *general* and state what a group has in common. They are a convenience, probably unique to the human; and they help organize things for understanding and memory, as well as for efficiency and prediction. In math, the same situation exists. Given the numbers 2, 4, 8, 16, 32, what is the next one in the series? This question can be answered only if the group of numbers is given a good set name or label.

Words themselves are also abstractions. The word *dog* does not wag its tail or bark at you from the page. The letter *p* does not spit or the letter *s* hiss. People have to learn that certain letter shapes stand for certain sounds and that these sounds combine to create other sounds. The spoken or written word is a convenience. That words are abstractions is further demonstrated by the fact that in different languages there are different words for the same thing; for example, *chien* or *hund* for dog. When words are used, there is a movement away from concrete experience. Often the smallest words like *it, is, a, the, to, for* are the most abstract. There is no picture to put beside these words.

When somebody *says* words, he helps the listener under-stand by the way he says them and by the expression on his face. Written words require signals like punctuation and capitalization. Paragraphs are indented to help the reader anticipate a new group of ideas coming up. Without this signal the beginning of the paragraph would not be noticed and the reader would not know to look out for the general topic sentence or the specific sentences belonging with it. When a category is written, the general label is also separated from the specific items by being capitalized and underlined or written larger.

Evaluation

After reviewing the vocabulary, knowledge of a few important concepts can be tested:

1. In a category the ___(label)___ tells you what the items have in common.
2. In a paragraph the __(topic___ sentence)_ introduces the reader to the main idea.
3. Topic sentences can be formed by using a category ___(label)___.
4. The way something is done is called the _(process)_.
5. Category labels are always _____(general, or abstractions)_____.

A valuable exercise involves finding in a room, and listing under an appropriate label, three or more items which can be heard, touched, or seen and which belong in one category.

A reading passage with comprehension questions may also be useful:

1. Any object, word, idea, event, or person can be categorized in several different ways. Each way will describe only a particular characteristic, not everything about the item. A full description would take many different categories.
2. Each category may be translated into a paragraph by using the label to make a topic sentence and the items for other sentences. Both the category label and the topic sentence will make a general statement about a particular group of items.
3. The process used to create categories and paragraphs is similar. Items are grouped, and a common characteristic is used for a general statement about their relationship. In textbooks, many paragraphs are based on categories; readers can find a label and specific items in them.

Questions

1. In describing categories, the word *item* can be used in place of
   a. objects
   b. words and ideas
   c. events or people
   d. a, b, and c.
      (*d* is correct)

2. A topic sentence should include specific items. True _____
   False __(√)__

3. Which paragraph tells you that a category can often be found within a paragraph?
   1. ___
   2. ___
   3. _(√)_

4. Choose the most suitable title for the three paragraphs above.
   a. Categories and Paragraphs
   b. How Paragraphs are Related to Categories
   c. All About Items
      (*b* is correct)

5. Label is to category as topic sentence is to __(paragraph)__ .

CHAPTER FOUR

Thinking in Categories

KEY VOCABULARY

aspect (-s)

relationship

degree

family tree

hierarchy (-ies, -ical)

superordinate

subordinate

inflexible (-ility)

prejudice

habit

similar (-ities)

difference (-s)

compare (-ing, -ison)

contrast (-ing)

patterns

outline (-ing)

numbering

lettering

consecutive (-ly)

positive

negative

KEY QUESTIONS

☐ Can all kinds of items besides objects be categorized?

☐ What are some other ways of using categories?

☐ What are some of the dangers of categorizing?

☐ Can any category be used to build a paragraph? Must all paragraphs be built this way?

☐ Can a category be broken into other categories?

☐ Can many categories be related in written units larger than a paragraph?

Preview of possible answers

All known or imagined items can be categorized, although it may not always be desirable to do so. Learning is facilitated by thinking in groups which may be compared and contrasted. Positive and negative aspects of subjects can be discussed.

There are dangers in categorizing since it is often done from insufficient observation or information. People also find it difficult to change categories, even when they find contradictory evidence, which leads to inflexibility and prejudice, or habitual ways of thinking which cease to be influenced by direct observation.

Any category about any topic can become a paragraph by translating the category label into a general, topic sentence, and using the specific items for the rest of the sentences. Paragraphs are not always written this way, however.

Any category can be broken down into other categories, all related to one another, and can be arranged like a family tree of ideas which can then be translated into a written unit larger than a paragraph.

Introduction

The scope of this part of the program is unlimited since it can become the basis of an interdisciplinary unit, with students experiencing the uses of categorizing in science, art, math, language study, social studies, physical education, industrial arts, home economics, and music. If the program is to be handled in this way, a simple introductory lecture can set the stage, and a summary at the end can tie ideas together. If, on the other hand, the classroom is a closed world, then considerably more time will have to be spent providing different kinds of experience. Teachers, parents, or persons in the community with special knowledge can be invited to demonstrate the use of categorizing in their fields. Students can work on projects of special interest (animals, cars, motorbikes, fashion, cooking, science, sports, art, and music). Any topic can help promote the seeing of patterns in the environment and communicating about them.

Teachers may want to enlist the aid of supervisors, department chairpersons, or principals in providing meaningful student experiences. Each community will offer different possibilities and limitations, just as students will have different needs. For all levels of students, there can be a challenge accompanied by pleasure if experiences are well planned. The deprived and low socioeconomic students are fully capable of understanding ways of making order and seeing patterns that are helpful. Gifted and advantaged students must learn a systematic approach and can benefit from instruction and demonstrations on how to deal with complex relationships.

☐ *Can all kinds of items besides objects be categorized?*

A good way to approach this question is through subjects the students are studying. How the subject matter will be used depends on the way this program is incorporated into the curriculum. As suggested in the introduction to this chapter, teachers from various disciplines can be enlisted, even if only informally. A survey of students' interests, hobbies, favorite television programs, or community activities can offer good starting points. Sharing small group projects and discussions may prove more fruitful than lectures. It is crucial that students do their own thinking and have plenty of opportunity to communicate these thoughts to others.

There are some rather easy ways of demonstrating the extent to which categorizing of widely different items is done in areas other than the classroom. The school library is an ideal place, and most librarians would welcome a chance to explain their system. The retrieval system using the card catalog fits with the earlier discussion on memory. Field trips to museums and galleries show relationships between categories. Each museum has certain goals, some rather limited; and, within the building itself, special rooms are usually set aside for particular categories, with similar objects being housed near one another. Art gallery divisions may be historical period and style. Students should be made aware of what to look for before the visit. A good lead would be to choose a particular room and make a category from observations.

In addition to everyday objects, museum pieces, and books, there are categories of people, events, and ideas and, in each case, the process includes observing, finding common characteristics, and labeling accordingly. Some of the problems involved are touched upon in the following pages.

☐ *What are some other ways of using categories?*

In the first three chapters of this volume, categories were described as being useful for surviving, understanding, remembering, predicting, being efficient, solving problems, and communicating. Another way of using categories is for comparing and contrasting. Unfamiliar objects can be observed and compared to known categories in order to know where to "file" them. Performance in school, in sports, or in many other areas is compared by using the categories of competition and achievement (Olympic Games, Academy Awards, or various school grouping and grading systems).

Categories are also used to organize ideas into hierarchies (familiar in school as outlining) and demonstrated in the tables of content of textbooks.

Comparing and contrasting

Incorporating the unfamiliar into an existing category system by comparing and contrasting was demonstrated in Chapter 1 with *Dogs, Dangerous Things,* and the banyan or baobab tree. Unfamiliar objects need to be observed carefully before comparison starts. Superficial observation leads to incorrect filing. For example, a seal is not labeled a dog just because it is heard barking. Some students might find it entertaining to think up similar examples.

Comparing and contrasting performance within categories is a daily occurrence. Consumer reports compare goods for shoppers by using specific criteria. Students evaluate course offerings and compare them before arranging their schedules. Spectator sports make statistics of performance a sacred rite.

Categories used to visually demonstrate comparisons are an important part of reporting today. *Graphs and charts* reduce process, performance, or opinion to limited areas and demonstrate comparisons within these areas. Graphs and charts are always an abstraction in their use of averaging techniques and are therefore removed from observable reality by one step. Carefully circumscribed observations are made of individual processes or people, but the final graph or chart represents averages and not the actual condition of any one process or person. Students in junior high are often confused about such calculations and even about how their own grades are averaged. Demonstrating the abstraction of categories used in reduced visual presentations, such as graphs, can help students read these more intelligently. The process is far removed from daily experience. The opposite process is the creation of labels on the basis of insufficient data. Three students are seen picking up trash outside a school and the observer generalizes: students today care so much about the environment that they even pick up trash. In this case, a generalization (label) is made on the basis of observation without taking the size of the sample into account.

Comparing categories involves two subdivisions: ways in which they are *similar* and ways in which they are *different*. A first reading assignment can be made to cover just two categories about any two subjects; for example, two different countries, historical figures, events, geographical areas, experiments, or works of art.

After taking notes under appropriate labels, students can make two statements: the subjects are similar in the following ways, and they are different in these respects. This process is an act of synthesis, or combining two aspects of a subject: the information itself and whether it falls in the *similar* or *different* category. These decisions need to be made by all students regardless of ability. Those who have a reading problem can use filmstrips or tapes and can dictate notes or record them on tape. Once the effort has been made, it should be evaluated carefully and further tasks planned.

Positive and negative views

The process of making decisions on the basis of comparing and contrasting categories, or items within categories, is very important and is often hindered by an inability to see both positive and negative sides of a question. As people mature, they must learn to be objective and to see other points of view, even on subjects about which they feel strongly. In junior high school, this process has hardly begun. Strong personal feelings often color student thinking. Some youths never outgrow this stage while others can be gently guided to see the advantages in understanding opposing viewpoints or the complexities of a situation.

One familiar area which clearly demonstrates complexities is ecology or environmental studies. Many students would like to have clean air and water, better trash disposal, and more open space. They also realize that bringing about changes to make these desirable things possible may lead to undesirable results, such as unemployment. What is the solution? More information, a careful weighing of all viewpoints, and probably some form of compromise are necessary.

The basic organization for making the kind of decision involved in school rules, environmental law, or even arrangements for a party is to list the pros and cons, or the positive and negative aspects. While students understand these terms in math or photography, they are often confused about them when dealing with language.

Brainstorming the words *negative* and *positive* can be a helpful beginning. The teacher might get things started by using the math signs and two words at the head of the columns, then accepting additions which should fall into categories such as feelings, conditions, and events. As the discussion continues, it may be possible to show places on a continuum, similar to a number line. Some words offered may be positive in one situation but negative in another. A useful concept for the discussion is the need for positive and negative electrical charges which form a power circuit in transistor radios and tape recorders. The idea of the circuit can be an analogy demonstrating the benefit of seeing both positive and negative aspects. The subject can be introduced by a student. The chalkboard should be arranged as follows:

COLLECTING IDEAS ABOUT THE WORDS

negative AND positive

Negative		Positive
—	-3 -2 -1 0 1 2 3	+
No	(maybe)	Yes

(After student contribution)

hate dislike (tolerate) like love
bad/unpleasant/(so-so)/pleasant/good

After brainstorming, it is wise to try a brief exercise with a topic of interest to all students, such as a dress code or discipline system. Groups can make lists of positive and negative aspects and then compare lists.

When the topical issue has been discussed, a particular passage can be read and examples from the content material can be worked on. Each student should do this exercise in an orderly manner. The paper should be headed *Positive and Negative Sides of the (X) Question* and divided into two columns. Once a number of items have been written by each student, a discussion can help them see what they have missed and allow them to add those items. Two ways of handling the information should be used. One way is to write a very brief introductory sentence: "There are two sides . . .," followed by a paragraph on the positive aspects, with topic sentence and items ordered logically, and the same for the negative aspects. (The emphasis should be on the structure rather than style.) When that is complete, one brief paragraph on three items, negative and positive, should be written, comparing both sides of an item in one sentence. The topic sentence for this paragraph would have to be something like, "There are positive and negative sides to the question of . . . ."

After this study of one question in depth, other examples in reading should be found and at least a two-column, positive and negative outline completed. If only one side is presented in the reading, students can be asked to think of or look for a few items to present for the other side. (Further comments on positive and negative aspects will be found in Chapter 9.)

Vocabulary study

School uses of categories for improving understanding and remembering can be demonstrated daily in any subject area. Creating a framework which includes new and familiar material is essential. This framework will usually consist of certain concepts basic to the particular area of study. Unless these are already firmly established in a student's mind, isolated items will remain isolated and consequently be forgotten or misapplied. Nowhere can this be better illustrated than in vocabulary. New words, if formally introduced at all, often are listed in random fashion with instructions to "learn" them. Students look them over and then read a textbook passage which includes the words. Students may be able to make the appropriate sounds for the words, but meaning escapes them. Later material assumes that the earlier has been understood. By this time, the students are lost.

Inadequate introduction of key words representing basic concepts leads to poor reading comprehension. The words look something like nonsense syllables, unrelated to familiar images. When beginning a new unit of learning, careful thinking is required. First of all, what underlying concepts are assumed? If maps are to be read, is every student familiar with the points of the compass and has he acquired mental images of coastlines, rivers, and mountains? Do students have mental maps of the school and neighborhood as points of reference? (Diagnostic information is sometimes available from analysis of standardized tests.) If history is the subject, can students place themselves in an historical framework? Many junior high students have no concepts of era, century, generation, decade, ancestor, contemporary, or descendant. Having each student create his own time line, from information·gathered at home, is an excellent task for teaching these concepts. Did a relative serve in a recent war? When did marriages and births take place? Can the student predict the point when he might change from being just a descendant to becoming an ancestor?

Once underlying concepts have been thought through, new vocabulary words can be divided into three groups. The first will consist only of words which are basic to all the other material, and each student must learn these words. Student-made review tapes and accompanying sheets can be helpful to students who have real problems. Ample class discussion and use of media other than reading are needed. Activities which involve using the words should be planned. The second group of words should be the borderline group (important but not basic). These words, including spelling, can be mastered by most students. The third group of words will concern important details which belong as subordinate items under the basic words. Students will learn these words much more easily in relation to the first list and should not encounter them in isolation. The industrial revolution can serve as an example:

Group 1   revolution
industrial - agricultural
inventions
interchangeable parts
power
factories - labor - cities
distribution - transportation
capital - surplus
communication
laws

These words all happen to be needed for reading the newspaper; they have to do with the whole fabric of modern society. Poor readers can work just as well on finding phonic patterns and known syllables, roots, and affixes within these words as in some list divorced from subject matter. *All* readers must be able to visualize something for each word. The pictures are made clearer by the second and third lists of words. For example: a student has learned that the word *transportation* consists of *trans* = across, *port* = carry, and the noun ending *-ation*. Now, he can form a category with *roads, railroads, rivers* and *canals,* and *ports.* The invention of the steam engine can be included as an improvement for transportation and cross-filed under inventions, industrial, and power.

When introducing vocabulary, the first requirement is that students be able to see the words clearly. Handwriting on the chalkboard or an overhead screen is seldom clear enough. The initial visual image of the word can help or hinder learning and it certainly affects spelling. Typewriters made for the early grades can be used to make transparencies, or a student who is good at printing can help. In addition to each word being clearly visible, grouping the words under a title and labels can be very useful. Here is one example:

44

SUB-SAHARA AFRICA

Important Rivers	Important Lakes	Types of Vegetation
Niger	Chad	tropical rain forest
Zaire	Victoria	savanna—tropical grassland
Zambezi	Tanganyika	tropical thorn forest
White and Blue Nile (upper reaches)	Nyasa	desert

In addition to being grouped for meaning, words can be grouped by spelling patterns. The basic words on the industrial revolution can be divided this way:

Words Beginning with Prefixes

*dis*tribution (the opposite of taking tribute)

    (*industrial* has no prefix as the root word includes *in*)

*in*vention (to arrive at something)

*inter*changeable (*inter* = between)

*re*volution (*re* = again + *volvere* = to roll)

*sur*plus (*sur* = over, above)

*trans*portation (*trans* = across + *portare* = carry)

Words Ending in Suffixes

interchange*able* (*able* = capable of, indicates an adjective)

agricultur*al* (*-al* usually indicates an adjective)

industri*al*

    (*capital* has no suffix as the root word includes the *al*)

distribu*tion* (*-tion* indicates a noun)

inven*tion*

transporta*tion*

y Changing to *-ies* for Plural Form

cit*y* - cit*ies*

factor*y* - factor*ies*

      It is even more desirable to have the students themselves make these categories in class discussion. The more ways a word is discussed, the easier it is to learn that word. Many students learn best through hearing; and emphasis on one part of a spoken word, spelling aloud in rhythmical patterns, or making verses with rhymes are all good teaching techniques. Visually, parts of the word, such as the root, can be capitalized.

A *vocabulary notebook* for any subject can be an important way of organizing study. Each page should have a main title and be divided into categories, with several lines left blank under each category for including words learned later. Vocabulary review and evaluation can be based on these pages. In the back of the notebook, pages can be set aside for listing spelling patterns and words with affixes. Many teachers are unfamiliar with these and should consult a reading teacher or an English teacher. Prefixes like *in-, com-, a-,* and *non-* always mean the same thing and students who know these can figure out meanings of unfamiliar words. In the same way, endings like *-ed, -ing, -s* or *-es* for plurals, and *-tion* indicate the function of the word and also help to reveal meaning. Analysis of this kind can make a word like *inter / change / able* easy. Columns assigned to each important affix can be used to list all new words containing that pattern. Review of these columns will do much to fix word-analysis techniques in students' minds. Every teacher will find a notebook of this kind helpful and a uniform, schoolwide procedure even more so. Carefully observing words, finding common characteristics among them, and labeling them accordingly are essential parts of learning.

Finding categories in reading material

Different techniques can be introduced once students are in the habit of consciously categorizing material. One technique is having students find items for a given label by reading. Making up labels for groups of familiar items *without* reading, then later checking in a book, is another technique. A third technique is presenting an incomplete category with a label and two items and asking for additional items. For example, the label *Important African Tribes* is given in addition to *Ashanti* and *Hausa*. Students then read to add items. This can be combined with subdivisions such as *West Coast Tribes* and *East Coast Tribes*.

As students become more skilled at thinking in groups, making up labels, and finding facts in their reading to fit labels or existing groups, more extensive tasks can be demanded of them. The class can make comparative summaries of two or three similar groups. After reading about and grouping African tribes geographically, students can choose three rather different tribes and read for information about history, beliefs, and customs. The facts can then be made into a chart with three columns and three boxes within each column. The act of organizing facts in this way helps students to remember. When another topic, such as the Middle East, is studied later, a more complex task can be required. After class discussion about important categories such as religion, history, language, and geography, students should take notes as they read in order to prepare for making an extensive review chart as the culminating activity of the unit. The best chart can be duplicated and used as the study guide for a final test. To prevent great frustration, there should be an evaluation of the chart *structure* and the titles of columns and boxes before all information has been written in. There may be several equally good arrangements.

□ *What are some of the dangers of categorizing?*

Giving a label to anything without careful and complete observation can have several unfortunate consequences. Although an item may be categorized in many ways, people often close their minds to other possibilities once they have made a decision. A person may simply be labeled "chubby" although he possesses many talents and good qualities. Categorizing can very easily become a negative activity. For example, students grouped by "ability" are often assumed to be in every way superior or inferior. In fact, the "inferior" students may have many talents, but they do not score high on one kind of test. Had it been left to schools to determine success in life, neither Churchill nor Einstein would have been heard from. Even if a student is a very poor reader, it cannot be assumed that he is stupid. He may have a perceptual problem; his family may have moved very often; he may have been seriously ill or suffered traumatic emotional experiences at a young age. Classes in which the same routines are followed day after day give no opportunity for discovering latent talent.

Prejudice

Limited categorizing, when applied to people, becomes prejudice. The answer to this is more categorizing rather than less. Previous activities should have demonstrated that categorizing anything one or two ways does not completely describe it. The chubby boy may always be neat and clean, have a wonderful sense of humor, and show a talent for drawing. Careful observation is again the key to good categorizing.

Poor judgment

A sense of judgment is involved in good categorizing. Items not only have to be grouped and labeled but also must be arranged in a hierarchy of importance. Experience and maturity are necessary for development of a sense of perspective, but exercises in ranking and selecting items can show the way. Observing how teachers and fellow students react to events and solve problems can provide students with models. There must be opportunities in the classroom for interacting, making decisions, and playing different roles. People's attitudes toward themselves and their environment greatly affect their ability to categorize. It may not be possible to radically change their perceptions, but demonstrating ways of approaching problems, giving students a sense of self-respect and worth, and providing each student with opportunities to succeed, can alter attitudes. Each student must develop his own categorizing system rather than try to use a teacher's system.

Students can be asked to make up or relate examples of poor item-ranking. Two examples follow.

1. Liz is invited to spend the night. Her friends take her out for dinner and the circus. Next day Mary asks, "Did you have a good time last night?" Liz replies, "It was okay, but can you imagine, the Smiths don't have color TV!"

This is equivalent to the category:

My Visit
Not having color TV
Going out to dinner
Going to the circus
Spending the night

2. John gets up every morning at five to practice running. At the final track meet he beats the school record for the hundred yard dash. Afterward, his aunt says to him, "You'd look better if you'd cut your hair."

This is equivalent to the category:

Aunt's View of John
Hair too long
Runs well
Practices hard

Other examples can be taken from the curriculum. Here are two examples of poor grouping:

1. Bodies of Water	2. Sources of Heat
oceans	the sun
lakes	fire
rivers	friction
puddles	matches

This subject will be dealt with more fully in Chapter 6.

☐ *Can any category be used to build a paragraph?*
  Must all paragraphs be built this way?

Any category can be used to build a paragraph by writing a topic sentence around the category label and using the items to create the rest of the paragraph. The topic sentence must fit the particular items in the category. For instance, if the items are basketball, baseball, and football and the label is *popular team sports,* the following topic sentence would not do at all: "Around the world, people enjoy many different popular team sports." To fit that topic sentence the items would have to be hockey, soccer, cricket, and polo, or a similar list. An adequate correction would be, "Popular team sports in the United States are basketball, baseball, and football."

All paragraphs are not built around categories. Many are made up of descriptive items, events, comments, and conversation without any topic sentence. Some compare two categories or discuss a cause and effect situation. Many are just loosely connected sentences. Well organized essays and textbooks include paragraphs with topic sentences built around clear categories. In novels and short stories, there may be very few categories.

☐ *Can a category be broken into other categories?*

Many categories can be broken down into more categories. Often each category item can become a label for another category. This process of category reproduction can go on and on. Earlier in this chapter, an example was given starting with *Sub-Sahara Africa,* and going through *African Tribes, West Coast African Tribes, Ashanti,* and *Tribal Customs.* The system can be seen most clearly in science. In zoology, for example, each organism can be classified by kingdom, phylum, class, order, family, genus, and species. Any table of organization for a military system or business enterprise demonstrates similar divisions and subdivisions.

Hierarchies

While the concept of category hierarchies is not difficult for adults to grasp, students emerging from a period of predominantly concrete, personal experience often find it very confusing. Links need to be formed between concrete experiences and abstract thought. One such link can be the study of family trees. (Care should be taken not to make the family tree too personal in order to spare students from embarrassment.) Historical figures or stories about interesting families are appropriate for classroom study. Three generations are necessary to make a tree on the chalkboard. Showing a name change through marriage is important, as related categories often have very different labels.

		John and Mary Smith			
	Freddy Smith			Louella Smith	
	married Katy Katz			married Ebenezer Dill	
Elizabeth	Francis	Mary	William	Joshua	Rebecca
Smith	Smith	Smith	Smith	Dill	Dill

In our society, family hierarchies do not always represent chains of command. An example of local significance should be chosen to illustrate this aspect of hierarchies. In addition to a local military installation, large enterprise, or government organization, the structure within a school can be used. Any example should be clearly illustrated.

Since the concept of categories spawning other categories is not easy to grasp, it may be wise to use a variety of examples. Some students will need numerous examples, while others will become interested only when a favorite topic is under discussion. In mathematics set theory, factoring and the metric system are related to this topic. Examples from science, such as the structure of atoms or the classification of a plant or animal, may arouse interest. Other possibilities are stock car racing or beauty contests. Students can gradually move from having examples presented as a whole to filling in the missing parts. Later, students can complete an entire representation of a chosen hierarchy.

As greater confidence is attained in organizing structures and understanding the meaning of hierarchy, the words *superordinate* and *subordinate* can be introduced. (Students may be familiar with *ordinal* numbers.) While it is not essential for students to learn the word *superordinate,* it can be helpful. The important part of the discussion is the concept of ideas embedded within other ideas, like sets of blocks which fit inside others. Further examples can be used from the categorizing of objects discussed in Chapter 2. Words like *color, texture,* and *shape* are superordinate to words like *blue, soft,* and *round.* The titles of the collections of objects (e.g., *Objects Categorized by Color*) are superordinate to the labels (*Blue Objects*), which are in turn superordinate to the items (candles). It might be wise to bring out the objects and display them under the titles and labels.

Relationships

1. *Family tree.* Combining categories inevitably brings up the word *relationship,* a very complex word. One value of using family trees as examples of hierarchies is that "my relatives" is a concept most people acquire early (although they may use "folks" or some other word). When relationship is discussed in family terms, it is not hard to explain different aspects of the relationships. Among generations there is a difference in *degree,* while male and female relatives represent a difference in *kind.* A grandfather/grandson relationship involves the same *kind,* but a difference of two degrees (generations). A grand*son* is two degrees *down* from a grand*father,* while a grandfather is two degrees *up* from his grandson. On the other hand, a brother/sister relationship involves different *kinds,* but the same *degree.*

2. *Analogies, opposites, cause and effect.* Besides family relationships, other varieties can be explored. Familiar ones may be analogies, opposites, and cause and effect situations. The amount of time spent on different types of relationships depends on the way this program is incorporated into the curriculum. If the students are in the seventh grade, care should be taken not to become too abstract. Endless duplicated sheets with disconnected exercises such as "red is to color as round is to _____," can be counterproductive. On the other hand, making up games around relationships seen in curriculum material can be very profitable. Chapter 9 deals with additional logical relationships.

3. *Changing values of items in different relationships.* Examples from art and music provide excellent ways of demonstrating the importance of the way things are combined. Observing a rehearsal of the school band will demonstrate the different values of notes played separately or in groups. The notes will again change value in different rhythms. Any band director can present this systematically. The same importance of relationship can be simply illustrated in the classroom by showing three differently colored sheets of construction paper, one of which is very light. At first, these sheets can be shown in different orders, across and up and down. After observing the effect of relative position, each student can make a collage out of one-third of a sheet of each color. This can be done as homework if preferable. No instructions should be given other than that all collages must be a previously agreed upon size (notebook size

is convenient). A gamut of relationships will be demonstrated if all collages are hung under the main title RELATIONSHIPS, with the subtitle *Collages Made of (Colors)*. Category labels can be used to subdivide the pictures by mood, predominant color, realism versus abstraction, or any other system chosen. Different labels which re-arrange the display can contribute further to understanding the complexity of relationships. The visual impression can be translated into language by asking the students to write brief, creative poems or prose pieces on the interaction of colors. The form of a haiku might be especially appropriate.

Changing values which are so important in art, music, and dance can be illustrated another way. As people grow up, they gradually learn to see themselves as a part of a larger environment instead of as the only important person. Additional layers of authority are added to the all-important parent or adult in the home. Getting a job means adding a whole system to the systems of home and school. During this process some things become much less important than they were at younger ages.

Acting out a skit can illustrate changing values in a few minutes. A group of students represent a team with a captain who should be the largest student or one wearing a sign. The group hovers around the captain who is clearly the Big Cheese. The coach then joins the group, which re-forms around him. The captain is obviously less important than he was. Voices are heard offstage and a small group enters surrounding a famous sports figure such as Hank Aaron. Everybody gathers around him and he clearly becomes the Big Cheese. Each central figure is diminished in importance with the arrival of the next person. The process can then be reversed.

4. *Different aspects.* The word *aspect* can be introduced while the collages are still in place. Many classroom teachers and textbook writers assume incorrectly that seventh or eighth grade students understand the concept of seeing a subject from different points of view. Their stage of development or experiences may not have conditioned them to do so. Different aspects need to be demonstrated in conjunction with a large model of the word *aspect* prominently displayed.

Pointing to the collages the teacher can say, "There are many different aspects of the use of color in these collages." A few students may be able to paraphrase this statement. A list of the different aspects should be similar to the list of category labels used for the display: color creates a mood, color can emphasize, color can create order or chaos, and color can be used to divide space. Students can be asked what aspect of color they were emphasizing when creating their collage.

A more direct representation of different aspects of one object can be created by drawing or pasting four very different pictures on the outside of a large carton. One student should sit directly facing each image and describe to the class what he sees. This act will illustrate the fact that a full and accurate description of an object from one point of view may not tell the whole story. A volunteer can be asked to describe this phenomenon. The answer might be something like "Four people have seen four very different *aspects* of this carton." The class should then be asked to discover other aspects. This could lead to four new aspects at the corners and one from the top. Each person of the last group of volunteers should preface his description of the carton by saying "From this aspect what I see is . . . ." Another volunteer can then summarize the activity by saying something similar to the following:

> We have seen that one object can appear very differently from different points of view. There was just one carton, but it had nine different aspects. These could be divided into three groups: 1) looking at the sides, 2) looking at the corners, and 3) looking from the top.

Students should then be asked to think up other aspects of the carton. A possible list would include: its shape, material, how it is put together, possible uses, and its dimensions. An outline of the whole discussion might look like this:

DIFFERENT ASPECTS OF THE CARTON

I. How it looks from all angles
   A. from the four sides
   B. from the four corners
   C. from the top
II. How the carton is made
   A. material
   B. dimensions
   C. method of construction
III. How it is used
   A. for transporting objects
   B. for storing objects
   C. for putting things on
   D. for a class demonstration

Careful observation and discussion have revealed many different aspects of the carton. When written out, there are ten items subordinate to three category labels, all under a superordinate title and all related to it.

A simpler demonstration can be sketched on the chalkboard. A three-sided mountain is pictured: 1) a sheer precipice; 2) a gentle, grassy slope with a stream; and 3) an irregular, rocky slope with trees. (This activity can, of course, be coordinated with geography study.) Three students are asked to describe the sides and another is asked to make a summary statement about the three different aspects of the mountain. Are there other aspects of this mountain? It can be looked at from the summit, from an airplane, or from a space ship; it can be described as to location, height, type of vegetation and possible animal life, economic factors, mountain climbing, and skiing. The summary might look like this:

DIFFERENT ASPECTS OF THE MOUNTAIN

I. How it looks from the surrounding country
  A. northwest side
  B. south side
  C. east side

II. How it looks from above
  A. from the summit
  B. from an airplane
  C. from a space ship

III. How it can be described geographically
  A. location
  B. climate
  C. elevation above sea level

IV. How natural resources can be described
  A. economic factors
    1. water power
    2. quarrying
    3. mining
    4. lumber
    5. crops or grazing
    6. tourism
  B. type of vegetation
  C. kinds of animal life
  D. water supply

V. How it can be used for recreation
  A. mountain climbing
  B. health resort
  C. skiing

This time sixteen items, with six further divisions under one of them, are organized into five subordinate categories under one superordinate title to which all are related. This illustration contains a "fourth generation" of relationship.

The next step in understanding the word *aspect* is to study a topical issue—a question of values or behavior not tied to any particular object. A school dress code or other rule, privileges at home, or something clearly within the experience of all students, should be chosen. An obvious place to start is with positive and negative aspects. Another aspect could be the way people in different roles (parents, the principal, or older students) might look at the issue. If a foreign country is being studied, then the point of view of a visitor from that country could be added. Yet another aspect is the relationship of this issue to other issues, such as the whole concept of authority or personal responsibility.

A final step in elaborating meanings of *aspect* is to find and list different aspects of a topic in reading. It should be pointed out initially that much of the work is done already in tables of content. Students might want to go to several sources to see if they can find different aspects. There is no need for reading lengthy passages, only headings and subheadings. The consensus should be that the phrase, *different aspects,* refers to a basic relationship between a number of categories under a superordinate label. Labels may be related to other labels in the way brother/sister or grandfather/grandson are related.

☐ *Can many categories be related in*
written units larger than a paragraph?

Any textbook organized into units, chapters, parts, or sections can illustrate the combining of categories into a large unit. After studying comparison and relationship, discussing the organization of more than one textbook should be meaningful to students. Spending a great deal of time learning a *system* of numbering and lettering should not be a primary concern. Emphasis on understanding the superordinate and subordinate relationship of one set of numbers or letters to another is more important. Each *set* represents one kind of category. In order to list all the items in one category, it is necessary to copy only headings next to consecutive numbers or letters. Finding the immediate superordinate label requires finding a heading with a different kind of number or letter. The student-built outline on *aspects* can be used to demonstrate this point. The numerals 1-6 are items in a category labeled *A*. *A* is one of a set of items *A-D* under a label numbered IV. These letters and numbers are symbols of the *types* of relationships involved.

Understanding the helpful aspects of organization, rather than its difficulties and complexities, can be stressed. The time saved in reading, if the organizational structure of a book is fully used, needs to be emphasized. The reading of every word is wasteful unless a person is looking for facts embedded in paragraphs. Unfortunately, some textbooks are not well organized and teachers need to be prepared to concede this point. Poor organization can make for wonderful learning opportunities: "It is true that the organization is bad; now, show me how it could be done better." Actual practice in answering questions from a table of contents, perhaps in the form of a game with teams, should convince students of the time-saving aspects of tables of contents, indexes, tables, and graphs. The structure of all frequently used books should be carefully investigated.

Conclusion

This chapter has dealt with concepts that are very complex. Many levels of understanding are involved. For the moment, the concern is to stay as close to the concrete world as possible while exploring abstract generalizations about it. All written material is itself an abstraction. For many students, this presents a sufficient obstacle to understanding without further complicating the learning process by using unfamiliar subject matter. Since understanding the organization of ideas is the goal, other difficulties should be eliminated if possible. If the foundation of understanding is firm and strong, organizational concepts will be gradually built up with growing intellectual maturity and increased experience.

Just as practice is important to the learning of physical skills, so there is great value in presenting many opportunities of different kinds for observing the workings of categorizing. These opportunities should be made meaningful by being connected to the lives of the students or by the subject matter being studied. Disconnected exercises in thinking skills are likely to create negative attitudes rather than increase understanding. In any case, success at isolated drills does not mean that a student is able to use the skills in practical situations.

Evaluation

If students have taken part in a number of activities described in this chapter or those devised by a teacher, evaluation should consist primarily of applications of techniques. These should be related as much as possible to the content area.

Instead of traditional vocabulary review methods, students can be asked to make up suitable questions about the key words. These should be answered by volunteers after being read aloud. Students should be reminded that the basic topic is THINKING IN CATEGORIES. All questions should be related to the main topic. For example, "What does the word *aspect* mean?" would not be a good question, while "Does seeing different aspects of a subject create a number of related categories?" would be.

If a teacher feels that making up questions is too difficult for a group of students, the following sample would serve after reviewing the words.

1. The way a person is connected to other members of his/her family is called a ___(relationship)___ .

2. The way the idea of *full* is connected to *empty, adding* to *subtracting,* or *yes* to *no* is called ___(being opposites, or positive and negative)___ .

3. If a person looks for *similarities* and *differences* between two things, he/she is ___(comparing, contrasting)___ .

4. The items *shark, electric eel,* and *killer whale* are ___(subordinate)___ to the label *Dangerous Water Creatures.*

5. "All students are lazy" is an example of (circle correct words): relationship, (prejudice), (inflexible categorizing), (poor observation), aspect.

6. Write the following under the correct heading, *superordinate idea* or *subordinate idea:*
   eagles, birds of prey, hawks, owls
   tables, chairs, desks, furniture

7. The President, Secretary of Defense, Joint Chiefs of Staff, generals, colonels, majors, captains, and lieutenants represent a (circle the correct words): aspect, (chain of command), (hierarchy), contrast, (special relationship).

8. Items numbered or lettered consecutively in a text all belong to the same ___(category)___ .

9. Rainfall, temperatures, prevailing winds, closeness to the equator, closeness to a large body of water, and altitude are ___(different aspects)___ of climate.

10. What word best expresses the relationship of the following groups of words to each other? They both represent ___(hierarchies)___ .
    principal   title
    teachers   category label
    students   specific items

If further work with the structure of textbooks is desirable, the following pattern of questions might be used:

1. Describe the hierarchy of ideas as shown in the table of contents. This means that you should see how the book is divided for clearer understanding.
   a. What are the main divisions called? (parts, chapters, units)
   b. What are smaller sections within the main divisions called? (sub-sections)
   c. How are the smaller sections shown in the text? (larger print, underlining, extra space)
2. Open the book to chapter (____).
   a. What is the title?
   b. How many main divisions of the text are there in this chapter?
   c. How are divisions within the main parts shown?
   d. Can you find any examples of numbering and lettering to indicate categories in this chapter? Give the page numbers.

Another form of evaluation would be connected with a project. Again, the purpose is to emphasize the concept of a hierarchy of ideas.

1. Write out the overall title of your main hobby or interest.
   _____

2. Look up your topic in the index volume of an encyclopedia. Choose one of the entries. (For example, look up *animals* and choose *wild, laws concerning*.)
   _____

3. Find the volume and page. How many paragraphs are under the heading? _____

4. Read *one* paragraph. Answer these questions.
   a. Is there a topic sentence, or general statement? Make a label out of it.
   _____

   b. Find and list three items that belong under the label.
   _____
   _____
   _____

CHAPTER FIVE

Writing Topic Sentences

KEY VOCABULARY

topic	title
sentence	vary (-iety, -iation)
general	style
specific	paragraph
indent (-ing, -ed, -ation)	relate (-d, -s, -ing)

KEY QUESTIONS

- ☐ What are the two parts of a sentence?
- ☐ What is the purpose of a topic sentence?
- ☐ What are the important requirements of a topic sentence?
- ☐ What are the parts of a topic sentence?
- ☐ What role does style play in written language?

Preview to possible answers

Written language usually groups sentences into paragraphs. Each paragraph has a particular purpose, and the sentences in it are all related to that purpose. In this chapter, only one kind of paragraph will be studied: the one most closely related to categories, with the topic sentence at the beginning.

The topic sentence alerts the reader to the subject of the paragraph and to the kind of specific ideas to be found in it. At the same time, the sentence relates the paragraph in some way to the title or the section or chapter. The topic sentence must be true, make a general statement, fit the specific items used in the rest of the paragraph, and be related to the title of the whole written unit. Besides fulfilling its function, the topic sentence should be written so that the reader wants to proceed and understands what to expect. It takes many years to develop a good style, but even a beginner can learn ways of varying topic sentences to make them more interesting.

Indentation serves as a helpful signal for starting a new group of ideas, a new paragraph. "Denting in" from the margin the first word in a paragraph visually alerts the reader to the need for finding a group of ideas different from that which went before.

Introduction

With this chapter, the writing activities begin. The ultimate goal is for each student to write a brief, one-page essay following a formal structure. This writing should help students to understand how expository, formal writing is put together and this knowledge should improve their reading. Before the essay is begun, each separate skill required in writing needs explanation and practice. Once the group has learned the parts, each student can proceed with the whole essay at his own speed.

Students whose language skills are inadequate may have done well on the categorizing exercises. This momentum should not be lost when writing begins. Two different approaches may be necessary. Many students learn well by working from models and practicing specific skills and only gradually generalize the skills in different situations. Some students, on the other hand, need to work backwards from understanding a whole scheme to working on individual skills.

One helpful indicator of the latter type of student, besides careful observation of classroom thinking activities, is the score on a nonverbal, abstract reasoning, standardized test. Quite frequently, students with verbal scores close to the bottom quartile have abstract reasoning scores in the top quartile. The nonverbal score indicates how good a student is at finding patterns in geometric shapes. Students who do well show a very real strength which is often overlooked. Just telling students that they have a very high, or even above average, score can do wonders for motivation. The student then knows that the teacher believes him to be bright in at least one area.

Students who are good at seeing patterns sometimes need to understand exactly how each skill fits into a particular product and why the product is worthwhile. All students, of course, should be told why they are asked to do assignments, but some must be told. Allowing them to suggest procedures and think up efficient systems can also be helpful. Teachers may believe they cannot take the time to deal with this kind of student in public school classes, but the alternative is often class disruption and frustration for all.

It is a mistake to assume that students who are poor readers are necessarily unintelligent. Some students suffer emotional stresses at home or in school or experience other disruptions in their personal lives. Some students also develop physically and neurologically later than others and have real perceptual problems in the early grades. These problems may include seeing incorrectly or reading from right to left. Such students do poorly in the early grades and teachers may categorize them as failures; they also may miss basic reading training. Teachers who work with students who have reading problems should look at each case very carefully. Genuinely slow students benefit from endless repetition of carefully structured tasks; other students may lose their last spark of interest through such a method. Resource teachers can help teachers assess the strengths of each student.

□ *What are the two parts of a sentence?*

Since an essential element of a paragraph is the sentence, a word must be said about student understanding of the basic structure of a simple sentence. (The final chapter will deal with the combining of sentences.) Some students reach the ninth grade without knowing when a sentence is incomplete, although all students are exposed to subject-predicate instruction. Students with this problem must receive help before they begin work on writing paragraphs. Since traditional instruction apparently has been unsuccessful with these students, other approaches should be tried. Physical movement combined with decision-making has sometimes been very successful where other techniques have failed.

Students must grasp the language concepts of noun-ness and verb-ness in order to express a complete thought. This is not to say that a group of words lacking either a subject or a verb makes *no* sense. In conversation, one or the other element is frequently omitted. Often the subject is clearly seen because of the context. Nevertheless, incomplete sentences can lead to serious misunderstandings and they should be avoided.

The two parts of a sentence must answer *"Who* or *what?"* and "What are they *doing* or *being?"* Students having problems might be encouraged to play a game together. This should be done standing up. Students take turns being the leader and holding a list of sentences: complete, lacking a subject, or lacking a verb, and the answer key. The others hold cards. In the right hand, the card says *"Who?/ What?"* In the left hand, the card says *"Doing?/Being?"* The leader reads a sentence. If students think it is complete, they stand still. If they think the subject is missing, they simultaneously hold up the *"Who/What?"* card and take the right foot off the floor. If they think the verb is missing, they hold up the *"Doing?/Being?"* card and raise the left foot off the floor. The purpose of standing on one foot is both to make the game more interesting and, fundamentally, to convey the idea that a group of words lacking one or the other suffers from being unstable. A student who has had problems with this concept for years is not going to be helped by a one-shot, ten-minute game. It may be necessary to repeat the game several times, starting with very simple examples and moving up to long groups of words. At least one-third of the sentences should be complete so students gain confidence in recognizing them. Later versions of the game would require that students supply the missing part of the sentence in such a way as to make a meaningful statement. (Workbook versions of this activity are certainly more convenient for the teacher, but they will be far less effective for students with real problems.) Early sentences should deal with concepts familiar to the students, such as subject matter that has just been covered extensively or episodes from class behavior: "_____ is always late," or "Manfred is _____ today." The leaders have to be able to read all the sentences. If this situation poses a problem, a student who reads well can practice with the poor reader ahead of time. There will be a real incentive to learn how to read the groups of words well.

☐ *What is the purpose of a topic sentence?*

After the discussions and activities of the preceding chapters, it should be possible to draw the answer to this question from the students. Probably the clearest way to do this is to write a title at the top of the chalkboard. On the left-hand side below the title, write a relevant category labeled 1. The specific items should be spaced so that the paragraph to be written on the right-hand side takes up about the same amount of space. Any topic familiar to all students can be chosen. For purposes of discussion the topic below will be used throughout this chapter, but it is not necessarily the best one for every group of students.

THE BASEBALL SEASON

(The first sentence should be underlined *after* discussion only.)

1. *Baseball Equipment*   There are several pieces of baseball equipment that we need in order to play a game. We cannot

    ball   play any game without a ball, bat,
    bat   mitts, bases, and a pitcher's mound.
    mitts

bases, pitcher's mound caps shoes protective equipment	Caps and rubber-soled shoes are necessary also. For formal baseball games, different kinds of mitts and protective equipment are needed as well.

The first order of business after writing the example will be to identify the topic sentence. How does one recognize a topic sentence? Does it correctly introduce the specific items? Does it contain the label or relationship of these items? Is it related to the title of the whole unit? Will the person reading the topic sentence have a good idea of what to look for in the paragraph that follows? In summary, then, the purpose of the topic sentence is to introduce the topic of the paragraph in such a way that the specific items will fit it and to relate the paragraph to the larger unit of writing.

☐ *What are important requirements of a topic sentence?*

This question can be explored with THE BASEBALL SEASON example still in view. Obviously, the purpose of a topic sentence and its qualities must be closely related. Qualities of topic sentences already implied are: 1) the topic sentence must be a clear statement of the general label, 2) it must introduce the specific items of the paragraph, and 3) it must help the reader tie the paragraph to the whole unit.

The topic sentence must also be true. Truth, in this context, means truth within the framework of each category. If the category is made up of imaginary items, like qualities of a good Hobbit, the topic sentence must be true in terms of that situation, not necessarily by real life standards. An example of a topic sentence that is not true would be to say, "Different kinds of protective equipment are necessary for *all* baseball games," followed by an itemized list of helmets, masks, and pads. One way of making a topic sentence untrue is to use the wrong determiner—all, none, some, a few, several, or many. "All junior high school students hate reading" is as false as "All junior high school students love reading." Discussing the use of qualifying words can introduce the students to the idea that the smallest word or part of a word, even an *s* or *ed,* can make a statement true or false.

Another quality of a topic sentence should be that people will want to read the paragraph. It takes many years to develop a good style or manner of stating ideas and even the most famous writers believe there is more to be learned about style. The primary concern of amateur writers must be topic sentences that function correctly. Later, there can be a concern for *form*. This order is best, not because form is less important, but because it is completely tied to function. The sentence must work in the paragraph. An elegant sentence that does not function is worse than useless, since it misleads the reader.

To illustrate the purpose and qualities of good topic sentences, the example, THE BASEBALL SEASON, can be expanded. After pointing out certain limitations, accept student suggestions for other categories that fit the title. The title is not as all-embracing as BASEBALL, nor as limited as BASEBALL PLAYERS. The word *season* has particular implications: a particular time, a certain kind of weather, possible association with joy at the long, school holiday, and our expectations as well as the trappings of the game itself.

Let us suppose that one of the categories suggested is *Feelings During a Baseball Game*. A small test of student understanding and attentiveness can be made. After writing the label, include items below it that do not belong and see what kind of reaction is generated. For instance, include these items: enjoy being cold, feel excitement about cheerleaders, and want something hot to drink. These items will doubtless be ridiculed instantly. Ask for a suitable label for them. Now erase the false items and write something like this:

Feelings During a Baseball Game

> waiting impatiently for some excitement
> feeling excited when there is a home run
> enjoying the sunshine
> wanting something cold to drink
> choking on the dust

Try an example of an untrue topic sentence: "Everybody has good feelings during a baseball game." This statement is untrue because the items are possible feelings, not attributable to everybody, nor does the sentence accurately reflect the specific items, some of which are negative. After discussion, try an example of a topic sentence that does not cover all the specific items: "People often get tired of waiting for something exciting to happen during a baseball game." The foregoing statement is not general enough to cover all the items, and it illustrates the hazards of mentioning specific items in the topic sentence. Another try might be: "I like to compare my feelings about baseball with my feelings about football." This sentence is much too general since it covers two categories. Also, if a person wants to write about his or her opinions or feelings, the first person must be included in the label: *My feelings about baseball.* At last a proper topic sentence can be attempted, like: "People have different kinds of feelings during a baseball game," or "There are different kinds of feelings we can have during a baseball game." When this category has been dealt with, proceed quickly to a third, numbered 3. The negative examples just used should help to speed up thinking on this last example.

☐ *What are the parts of a topic sentence?*

Every sentence needs to have somebody (or something) doing or being something. This is not a rule made up by language teachers, but rather one dictated by the way people's minds work. If someone says, "Went along the road," somebody else is going to ask, *"Who* went?"; or if the statement is made, "The principal everybody for the good science fair," the reader or listener will ask, "What did he *do?"* The subject to use in a topic sentence will be determined by the sense of the category, or it may only imply a subject. In a general sentence like, "People have different kinds of feelings during a baseball game," it is safe to use the subject *people,* because it is obvious that the category is about human feelings. There is also the possibility of using *we,* in the sense of "people in general." People could also be implied by saying, "Different feelings are possible during a baseball game," using *feelings* as the actual subject. Another choice would be, "Spectators have different feelings during a baseball game."

There will be many occasions when the subject will have to be qualified by words such as *some, a few,* or *many* in order to make a truthful statement. This is especially true of collective words like *people, Americans, students,* or *birds.* It is almost never true that all of a large category share more than one attribute. (It is true to say, "All birds have wings," but untrue to say "All birds can fly.") If there are 200 million people in a category, and *one* of them does not agree with an opinion, it is untrue to say, "All northern Chinese like snow."

The verb will also have to be thought about carefully in relation to the category. Basic considerations will be whether the subject is singular or plural and whether the action took place in the past, is taking place now, or will take place in the future. Before choosing a limited verb, a careful check of the items needs to be made. For example, *explored* shows an intentional search, whereas *found* can cover either intentional or unintentional discoveries. The diamond rush in southern Africa was started by the accidental *finding* of a huge diamond, after which the area was *explored* for diamonds. *Went* may fit all the items better than *walked* or *ran* or

65

drove. The search must be for a word that is general enough without being too broad.

There may be a need to "make up" a verb for a category, in the same way that *people* was selected as a suitable subject for the category on feelings. This is especially true if the verb has to imply being rather than doing. Thinking back to categorizing the objects, it will be recalled that one category is *soft objects.* These soft objects were not doing anything. Some form of the verb *to be* is appropriate. The way it was handled originally was to say, "There are a few soft objects." If the category label is *Causes of the American Revolution,* "there were" will be suitable.

In the interest of truthfulness, the verb sometimes will also have to be qualified by words like *sometimes, usually,* or *occasionally.* Again, this will be necessary whenever there is uncertainty about the subject *always* doing or being something. If there is any doubt, it is better to qualify the statement since this is essential for truthfulness.

Having taken care of the subject and verb and qualified them, if necessary, there usually needs to be another part of the topic sentence which provides information on time or space or establishes a connection with the title. This part of the sentence will answer the questions: Where? When? What for? If the sentence reads, "There are a few soft objects," the reader is left hanging. The sentence is completed by saying, "in this collection," or something similar. In THE BASEBALL SEASON category on equipment, the statement, "There are several pieces of baseball equipment," was followed by "which we need in order to play the game." If it suits the purposes of the category or the whole unit, the time may be limited. Depending on the items chosen, the topic sentence on *Causes of the American Revolution* may be completed by saying, "In the third quarter of the eighteenth century," or "between 1750 and 1776."

It is possible, then, to have a basic formula for a topic sentence to help students construct true, general statements which introduce the items correctly and tie the paragraph to the title of the whole unit. The words *there are* (were, will be, may be) followed by a determiner like *some, many, a few,* or *several* qualifying the subject of the category, may be followed by a phrase establishing the *where, when,* or *what for* aspects of the category.

verb	determiner	subject	completing phrase
There are/	a few/	soft objects/	in this collection.
There were/	many/	important events in 1774/	which led to the American Revolution.
There are/	some/	people/	who like to pop balloons/ at parties.

Studying the topic sentences written for the object categories and the three written for THE BASEBALL SEASON, all of which are familiar to the students, may be the best way of introducing the idea of the formula topic sentence. This needs to be only a quick introduction. The next step should be the writing of formula topic sentences to go with categories derived from the curriculum. A very important part of this practice will be an extremely careful selection of the category labels. Some of these should be given and others should be worked on by the students. Topic sentences written on vague or inaccurate category labels are unsatisfactory. Reading can be useful again at this point. Research may be necessary to establish the truth of a category label. As an example, the category *Australian Songbirds* (including the items bell magpies, bowerbirds, and birds of paradise) may be checked in an encyclopedia to make sure the birds do not also appear in other locations.

Deliberate errors again can be used in order to illustrate the importance of careful thinking about the subject, verb, their qualifiers, and the completing phrase. Throughout all the discussions and activities of this program, a system of rewards for detecting errors should be in effect. Teachers need not be embarrassed about occasional errors, since every living being is subject to a mistake once in a while. Errors by group members can be useful learning tools, whether they are deliberate or unintentional errors. Rewarding the detection of errors can be a useful way of keeping the attention of the group. Students should not be penalized if they think there is an error where none exists, or they will soon give up taking risks. Taking risks is such an essential part of this whole program that it needs to be encouraged in every possible way. It is, of course, equally important to correct errors before they have entered the system.

Marking a topic sentence *wrong* accomplishes nothing unless a student understands what is wrong and why it is wrong. It is, therefore, most profitable to have students read their topic sentences to a group and have the others comment on it. Students who show a real grasp of the formula can be of great help to others at this point.

In practicing topic sentences, students need a wide variety of categories to be prepared for different situations. Examples are: 1) very limited or very extensive groups of people; 2) scientific facts; 3) symbols; 4) emotions and sensory impressions; 5) controversial subjects such as religions, minorities, or school discipline; and 6) chronological events. Disagreements on these sentences can lead to profitable checking in reference books. In the discussion, there should be possibilities of referring to earlier aspects of the program, such as different ways of categorizing, careful observation, inflexible categorizing, and the uses of categorizing for learning and remembering.

□ *What role does style play in written language?*

Style, manner, or form of writing has everything to do with helping a reader to understand the material and to want to read it. Long, confused sentences are difficult to follow. On the other hand, an endless stream of very short, simple sentences becomes boring and sleep inducing. Variety is essential for holding the attention of the reader. No tennis player intent on winning will serve the same way to the same spot every time. The element of the unexpected is very important. (Chapter 9 continues this discussion.)

The useful formula for writing topic sentences can be used in actual writing. Often the sentence will have to be altered but without sacrificing any of the essential elements. There are standard ways of varying the formula topic sentence; and it is helpful to review the most familiar formula sentences (for example, the objects, THE BASEBALL SEASON), showing at least two ways of altering each.

Formula topic sentence: (verb first) There are a few soft objects in this collection.

Placing the subject first: A few soft objects are in this collection.

Rounding out the sentence for a better, or more sophisticated style: A few soft objects are to be found in this collection. In this collection a few soft objects are to be found.

Further individual practice can be done on the curriculum-connected formula sentences which have already been checked. If these are placed four or five lines apart on notebook paper, and the variations are written in below, the corrected sheet can become a handy reference tool for the individual essay. A very important point is making sure that all sentences are indented. This may look odd when there are only topic sentences on the page, but it is part of building a good habit of thought. "Paragraphs normally start with an indentation." There are other ways of signaling paragraphs in print, but indentation is best for writing.

Conclusion

The desired result of the activities of this chapter is a realization by the students that language is purposeful. In behavioral terms, the expected outcome is greater precision in handling language and understanding that different language structures have different functions. A topic sentence must include a carefully chosen and qualified subject; a verb that suits the subject and the items in the category; and a concluding phrase which ties the sentence to the main subject and establishes time, place, or purpose.

We learn to write well through extensive experience in writing, wide reading, careful development of vocabulary, and broad acquisition of knowledge about the environment. Our main concern is the proper functioning of the language used, followed by attempts to create appeal through style and variety.

Evaluation

It will not be necessary to review the vocabulary of this chapter since the only new word is *style,* and that will be discussed further.

Learning about topic sentences can be evaluated by presenting a carefully considered category on a topic understood by all the students and asking for a topic sentence written according to the formula, followed by two variations of the formula. A complex category is not a good test for all the students, but it may be added as an extra credit item. Part of the test could be criticism of an incorrect topic sentence for a given category and a list of the reasons for the criticism. Another valid procedure is to quote topic sentences already read in a text and ask students to anticipate some items in the succeeding paragraph. This procedure should be self-checking in the text.

The evaluation should be so structured that every student can avoid failure. A feeling of being able to cope is essential throughout the writing activities.

CHAPTER SIX

Completing Paragraphs from Specific Items of Categories

KEY VOCABULARY

specific items	chronological order
arbitrary order	sequence
numerical order	cause and effect relationship
alphabetical order	subcategories
logical order	

KEY QUESTIONS

☐ Can specific items of a category be used for completing a paragraph after the topic sentence has been written?

☐ How are the specific items chosen?

☐ How are the specific items arranged in order?

☐ What do we mean by logical order?

Preview of possible answers

Once the topic sentence of a paragraph has been written, based on the category label, the paragraph can be completed by basing sentences on the specific items of the category. These items sometimes will be a list which must be presented in its entirety. At other times, there will be too many items for a paragraph and choices will have to be made. Those items included in the paragraph must be carefully chosen according to the purpose of the paragraph and the whole, written unit. The items also must be presented in a logical order.

Introduction

On one level, the completion of a paragraph from the specific items is relatively simple, given the topic sentence. It is not hard to complete a paragraph on *Baseball Equipment,* with a limited list of items of a finite nature. On another level, the completion of a paragraph can be of enormous complexity, involving implications of cause and effect, subtle subcategories, or personal bias. The fact that problems such as these exist needs to be discussed, while actual initial writing practice is confined to simpler categories. The mechanics of paragraph construction need to be studied first before worrying about shades of meaning. Again, as with the writing of topic sentences, students should realize that good writing is a matter of maturity, education, and opportunities to practice.

In attempting to develop a system for organizing ideas in written form, the real complexities are not ignored, only postponed. The foundation must first be firmly constructed to then support a variety of superstructures.

☐ *Can specific items of a category be used for completing a paragraph after the topic sentence has been written?*

Items in a paragraph built from a category can be used to complete it, given a topic sentence. This was demonstrated in the paragraph on *Baseball Equipment* in Chapter 4. Any category of strictly factual, concrete items can provide the parts for a straightforward, correct, and functioning paragraph. Even a highly theoretical paragraph can be organized around a category just as a highly complex painting can be based on a few simple geometric forms.

☐ *How are the specific items chosen?*

The label *Baseball Equipment* was an example of a limited topic. It was possible to list all major equipment in one paragraph, even though greater detail might have been provided in a longer discussion. There are, however, many other topics which cannot be covered, even in broad outline, in one paragraph without greatly reducing the number of items to be included. In a textbook on U.S. history, for example, the authors may feel the need to mention an event such as the Whiskey Rebellion in one paragraph without going into great detail. The items for such a paragraph will have to be chosen with great care since a whole book could be written on the subject.

Just as categories can reproduce other categories, so can many subcategories be reduced either to their labels or to one or two representative or especially important examples. Given a long list of possible items, a writer can sort them into categories with appropriate labels; then he can decide whether he wants to include all categories and whether he wants to use the label of the subcategories or an item or two from each group. For example, a subject such as

THE FOUR SEASONS will call for the category *Spring*. A writer can list many things associated with this topic:

warm	green	birds singing
rain	blue	school is a jail
light earlier and later	pink	wanting to travel
Easter	yellow	Passover
dyeing eggs	perfume	Ides of March
rabbits	smell of fertilizer	new clothes
blue skies	sound of raking	kids yelling
flowers	bags of trash by the road	baseball

By grouping, the author might reduce this limited list to the following subcategories:

sounds of spring
sights of spring
smells of spring
changes in the neighborhood
special feast days
emotions
activities

Obviously, there are still too many aspects to discuss in one paragraph. Can any of the subcategories be combined? Sounds, sights, and smells can become *sense impressions*. Activities and changes in the neighborhood can also be grouped together. That will leave these labels:

sense impressions
activities
emotions
special feast days

Using the most elementary writing technique, the following paragraph is possible:

There are several special things about spring. Our senses tell us that the season is changing. Daylight comes earlier. Birds sing, kids yell, and flowers are colorful and fragrant. We see people working in the yard, chatting with neighbors, playing baseball, and riding bikes. Schools become jails and we long to get out and travel. Everybody seems to wear new clothes, especially for feast days such as Passover and Easter.

This paragraph may not be exciting, but it works. Almost any student who can write at all can manage something like it by working with the system described.

The same original list of items can be used differently by selecting contrasting elements rather than using subcategory labels:

> Spring is a season of contrasts. The green leaves and grass and the bright flowers look so cheerful in the bright sun, but suddenly the sky is dark and it rains and rains. We smell the perfume of apple blossoms and daffodils and then the sharp smell of fertilizer. School seems like a jail while out there the whole world is waiting for us.

The choice of items, the way the paragraph is constructed, and the style will depend on the author's purpose in the whole unit called THE FOUR SEASONS.

Chapter 6 deals with brainstorming for ideas, and students have further practice in thinking up ideas as they write essays. For the moment, therefore, practice in using given items will be most helpful in understanding how to complete a paragraph once the topic sentence is written. The items, however, will have to be used in some kind of order. Therefore, the question of logical order must be taken up before writing practice can start.

☐ *What do we mean by logical order?*

Students are most familiar with two types of order: alphabetical and numerical. Alphabetical order often has been especially emphasized because of its uses in finding references or words in the dictionary. Roll is called in alphabetical order. Numerical order is used for random grouping in gym classes or at camp. Questions are numbered. Chapters in books are numbered.

Logical order is different from alphabetical order, often different from numerical order. This can be shown by example. List three or four wild animals alphabetically.

Wild Animals
elephant
monkey
zebra

Ask the students whether this alphabetical order lends itself to discussing the animals in a sensible way. What about the sizes of the animals? What about the natural habitats of the animals? What about their food? Whichever topic is discussed, it will be found that monkeys do not fit in between elephants and zebras. One form of logical order (size) would be to list monkeys first and elephants last or vice versa. Another form of logical order would be to separate monkeys as living in tropical forests, while elephants and zebras live on the savanna. Yet another order would be a division on the grounds of diet. In no way does the alphabetical listing make sense.

Many similar examples are available within the curriculum of the moment. Teachers need to think carefully about their choices before presenting them since there are many different ways of ordering logically. No student should be penalized for doing it differently, provided he has a good reason. With the example on wild animals, for instance, one student came up with the idea of listing according to frequency of appearance—a perfectly logical procedure.

Chronological order

A very important concept is chronological order which may be obvious to adults but not at all obvious to many students. Perhaps student concept of time is different; they have not yet filled out forms listing events in their lives chronologically. In any case, students require experiences that reveal the need to list certain items in chronological order. Here is a category listed in alphabetical order:

The School Day
English
Industrial Arts
Lunch
Math
Music
Physical Education
Science
Social Studies

Ask students to criticize this list. They may point out that everyone will be eating lunch at about ten o'clock and that most schools do not have eight periods a day. In addition, art and home economics have been omitted. Above all, this alphabetical order will not fit the actual chronological order of the school day for any student in the class. The alphabetical listing is purely arbitrary. Other examples of chronological order familiar to students might be holidays celebrated during the year, including Jewish holidays and Martin Luther King, Jr., Day. Alphabetical listings would put Christmas at the top of every list, whereas the holiday comes last in the calendar year.

Within the Christian church year starting at Easter, Christmas again comes near the end.

Geographical order

Geographical order is another type of order which fits with the curriculum. Whether the Middle Atlantic States or the countries of Africa, South America, or Asia are chosen, alphabetical order makes no sense geographically. To make this type of order more concrete, have students describe a trip through three or four states or countries. Such a description involves careful examination of physical and political maps and requires investigation of climate and communication. One does not casually drive from India through Nepal to China, for example. For students with very limited travel experience, neighborhood examples should be used at first. Obstacles such as walls, rivers, or freeways should be included. Students who have traveled can prepare an oral description of points along the way on a particular trip.

Sequence

Geographical order involves aspects of sequence, the next system of order which should be discussed. An excellent way of demonstrating to students is to have them write directions for one another, describing simple tasks within the classroom. Each direction should be written on a separate slip of paper and placed in random order. Another student should at first attempt to follow the directions in jumbled order and then make the necessary adjustments.

Cause and effect

Sequence and chronological order often involve elements of cause and effect. Below are four examples of cause and effect situations listed in the wrong order. Many examples can be found from recent events in the classroom or the community, known to all students.

1. The crowd cheered. Mary hit a home run with the bases loaded.
2. The car exploded. Mr. Williams lit a cigarette while syphoning gas.
3. The teacher praised Freddy. Freddy did his homework and handed it in on time.
4. World War I began. The Archduke Ferdinand was assassinated.

Chapter 9 deals with words (such as *because*) used to convey cause and effect sequences.

Given a topic sentence at the outset, practice in filling in specific items in logical order should include categories familiar to every student. These categories can come from daily life or from the curriculum, provided each student understands the subject matter. After a student has shown familiarity with the process of completing simple paragraphs, he can proceed with less familiar categories involving some research or he can attempt to create categories with topic sentences for other students to finish.

Before completing paragraphs, students should review the necessary process involved: 1) Look over the whole category. 2) Read the label and topic sentence carefully. 3) Decide on the logical order of the items (by chronology, geography, size, sequence, possible cause and effect, or other order). 4) Choose a tone for the paragraph (factual, humorous, fanciful or poetic).

The following examples are some of many which could be selected from daily life or school curriculum.

Example 1 (This is the only example already in logical order.)

Getting Ready for School

Alarm rings
Not wanting to get up
Not being able to find the
   right clothes
Rush through breakfast
Collecting lunch or lunch money,
   notes, and homework

Every school day there is a rush to get ready for school.

Example 2

South American Countries–West Coast

Colombia
Chile
Ecuador
Peru

There are four countries along the west coast of South America.

Example 3

Human Beings Growing Up

Being born helpless
Falling in love
Learning to walk
Going to school
Learning to talk

Human beings grow up the same way no matter where they live.

Example 4

Sounds at Night

Dogs barking
Footsteps
Police cars
Rustling
Cats meowing
Creaks on the stairs
Owls hooting
Fire trucks

At night when you lie in
bed, you can hear all kinds of
noises.

Example 5

Homes

Tents
Mansions
Apartment buildings
Cottages
Town houses

Most people have some place
they call home.

Conclusion

The important task of this chapter is to help students become aware of the various organizational factors involved in constructing a workable paragraph from a category and a topic sentence. Although it is helpful to think in categories, merely listing specific items in an arbitrary or random fashion is not enough. The inner logic of the subject must be made clear through the order of the items and the suitability of sentences built around the items. A paragraph must house ideas suitably, just as a building must be constructed to serve as a home or an office and not merely look grand. An ornate front porch will not offset narrow, dark hallways within; and three-syllable verbiage does not necessarily shed light on meaning. Form and content must be coordinated. Beyond that, a writer may want to introduce humor, propaganda, or personal bias. These aspects of the author's purpose also influence the form as revealed by the choice of language. One or two words can slant an entire paragraph. Chapter 9 discusses this further.

A reverse process takes place in reading. The reader must find the category label, either as given in the topic sentence or as implied by the whole paragraph; and he must identify the specific items embedded within the sentences. The relationship of the whole paragraph to the larger unit must be noted. The tone will reveal the author's purpose. Eventually, students should be able to use their understanding of organizational patterns to evaluate what they read.

Evaluation

Simple paragraphs from texts used in class can be used for reading evaluation. A brief form is helpful for guiding students and for checking their progress. An example follows.

Name of book _____ Page ____ Paragraph No. ____

1. Write the first three words of the topic sentence, if there is one. __
   _____

2. Turn the topic sentence into a suitable label, or make one up if there is no topic sentence. _____

3. List specific items you find in the rest of the paragraph.
   _____
   _____
   _____

4. What is the title of the whole section? _____

5. Write a one sentence summary of the paragraph in your own words. Discuss it with a friend before handing it in. _____

6. What system is used to order the items? (size, value, chronology, geography) _____

Here is a simple paragraph reduced to a category given as an example.

CAMPING

Camping makes most people really hungry, and maybe that is why campfire cooking smells so good. First, there is the smell of burning wood, sometimes mixed with more than enough smoke. Bacon, chicken, steak, and hamburger sizzle and make delicious aromas. Fried fish is good too. If potatoes are buried in the hot coals, they smell wonderful after an hour or two. Toasted marshmallows are fine, unless they get burned. Just thinking about these smells can make a person hungry!

This paragraph can be reduced to:

The Smells of Campfire Cooking
      Wood
      Smoke
      Bacon
      Chicken
      Steak
      Hamburger
      Fish
      Potatoes
      Marshmallows

Evaluation of writing would be done logically by presenting, under controlled conditions, another example of a topic sentence with specific items and by asking for a completed paragraph. The test category should be on a familiar subject, and the topic sentence and items should be read aloud before writing begins.

CHAPTER SEVEN

Collecting and Organizing Ideas for Writing

KEY VOCABULARY

association of ideas	comparison
experience	contrast
sense impressions	cause
emotions	effect
symbol (-s, -ic)	concentration
different meanings of words	analysis (analyze)
research	appropriate
brainstorming	

KEY QUESTIONS

☐ Are there reliable ways of collecting ideas for writing?

☐ How can ideas be organized for writing?

☐ What is the purpose of having an introduction and a conclusion?

Preview of possible answers

There are systematic ways of collecting ideas for any piece of writing, although writers do not always approach the task in the same way. Personal records of famous writers, such as Hemingway or Dickens, reveal that writing is mostly hard work and that each writer develops his own system.

Once ideas are collected, they can be organized into categories which represent units such as chapters, sections, or paragraphs.

The writer will often help to set the tone and purpose of his work with an introduction. He will often sum up the ideas in a conclusion.

Introduction

The discussion and activities that follow are a rehearsal for individual essays and for other activities outlined in Chapter 8 and should be practice sessions rather than isolated assignments. Careful review of procedures and evaluation of student work will lead to smoother and more successful individual writing. Student questions need to be encouraged. Fellow students are often able to answer queries.

The order of the procedures that follow is not important. Student suggestions can be accepted in any order. Only during review is it wise to place research last on the list, since students need every encouragement to think for themselves and make their own contributions. Research is more meaningful when it fills recognized needs or when the student is blocked.

□ *Are there reliable ways of collecting ideas for writing?*

Contrary to popular belief, art is mostly hard work. Writing on any level is a craft which has to be learned. This learning comes about not only from trying to write but also from noticing how others do it, whether they are professional writers or fellow students. An aspiring fashion designer studies fashion magazines and analyzes what brings success. Someone who wants to be an auto mechanic watches a professional mechanic repair cars and asks questions. Careful observation and the ability to analyze how things work is as important to good writing as to any other craft. Reading and writing go hand in hand.

In the previous two chapters, students concentrated on topic sentences and the use of specific items. In this chapter, the emphasis will be on procedures for collecting and organizing ideas.

Using association of ideas

One idea often leads to another. If someone says "hamburger," another may add "french fries." The word *salt* can trigger development of a long list of spices. When reminded of something by a word, sight, sound, smell, taste, or touch, people are associating one object or idea with another. (This is discussed in Chapter 1 in connection with a trip to Africa or Asia.) Association of ideas is one of the easiest ways to gather material for writing although many of the items may not be used in the final writing. The best ideas will have to be selected.

Tapping personal experience

Once inside the school walls, many students shut out the world beyond. When gathering ideas for writing, it is fatal to limit the area of search to the classroom and library. Most students have watched thousands of hours of television and have seen all kinds of programs. Most of them have also traveled beyond their immediate community. Some students remember what they have read on their own. All of these relevant experiences should be retrieved from the memory file. If the topic is *Bridges,* the student can remember all the different kinds of bridges he has seen or read about. This information can be used as a starting point and as a check when looking for other information.

One reason why students do not use their experiences is that they are not often encouraged to do so. To them information appears to have little value unless it comes out of a book. This situation automatically excludes poor readers from discussions.

One might approach new topics by dividing students into groups and asking them to pool information they may have before they look in books. After time for discussion, the groups can share their information with the class. Even if very little information is available, students can try making up questions. For instance, if the topic is *The System of Checks and Balances,* they can begin by trying to define the words *system, checks,* and *balances* and by thinking about their relationships. What kind of mental image is appropriate, if any? Having gone as far as they can without books, groups should think about possible places to find information. Once the class agrees about areas of investigation, the teacher or group leaders can assign individual students to look up specific aspects and report back. In this way, student thinking and experiences are valued, and the ideas contribute to decisions about reading tasks. No student is discouraged by having to read pages and pages without understanding what he is looking for.

Using sense impressions

Real-life categorizing starts with the senses (Chapter 1). Impressions must first be received before they can be grouped. When writing, it is important to think about sense impressions. They will provide many ideas which will help the reader visualize a scene imagined or described by the writer. If *Swimming* is the topic, thinking about sense impressions may provide ideas such as cold water; the smell of chlorine; breathlessness; echoes from shouting people;

the sound of waves; salty, stinging scratches; and muddy feet. Sense impressions are excellent tools for association of ideas. Aspects such as temperature, degree of light, odors, and contact with objects or people are present everywhere and every student can think and write about them.

Using emotions

Sense impressions often create emotional reactions. The howl of the fire siren creates excitement or fear. The heat of the sun may cause a comfortable, lazy feeling or produce paralyzing thirst. In fiction, much of the excitement is created by describing people's emotional reactions to events. Students have experienced joy and sorrow, love and hate, envy and contentment, fear and confidence, excitement and boredom; they can use their own reactions to understand the emotions of others. Every event stimulates emotions of some kind which could range from mild likes and dislikes to extreme anger, fear, or love.

Using or interpreting symbols

In every culture, there are symbols used to express ideas, inspire patriotism, sustain religious faith, or communicate rapidly. Africans and American Indians use drums and smoke for signals; others employ the Morse code; letters become symbols for sounds; traffic signals inform us. Cars and clothing can be symbols: the Cadillac and the Volkswagen, well-cut business suits, and blue jeans are symbols of generations or degrees of wealth. Certain words have a symbolic meaning far beyond their practical meaning (*Watergate*). Many topics have symbols associated with them or words that must be used with special care. *Black* and *white* represent more than color in our society. Thinking about symbols is more difficult than recalling experiences.

Using different meanings of words

Many words have different meanings, and these clues can be used to expand ideas for writing. *Pole,* for example, can be a terminal point such as North Pole; it can refer to someone from Poland, to people with very different opinions, or just to a post. A dictionary of synonyms can demonstrate the many meanings a word can have. These different meanings can enrich writing.

Comparing and contrasting

Another way of collecting ideas for writing is to use comparison and contrast. Comparison may help explain new material to the reader; for example, a desert may be compared with a known beach. Contrast can arouse the interest of the reader as well as help to explain. A dictionary of antonyms can be a good starting point. Excellent examples appear in the daily newspaper. For instance, the style of the President can be contrasted to the style of an earlier President. In another case, the contrast might be between expectation and realization. Mrs. Mudd goes to the bank to take five dollars out of her savings account and becomes a hostage in a holdup. A crowd goes to a ball game expecting a fine evening but is caught in a cloudburst. At school, students arrive worried on the day of a big test but are relieved to learn it is postponed. Most people experience extremes of temperatures indoors and outdoors, in summer and winter. These comparisons and contrasts can add a great deal of interest to writing.

Thinking about cause and effect

Many things can be both cause and effect, and thinking about them can add ideas for writing. Heat, for example, can cause fires, cook food, or keep us warm; but heat can also become an effect of friction, burning fuel, or the sun. Rain falls because of moisture condensation, but it also causes things to grow.

Doing research

Once a writer has dredged up every bit of information he already has on a subject, he may feel the need to search for more. Through research he can gather factual, descriptive material and historical information.

Finding descriptive material. Using category headings, a writer can find information in indexes, tables of content, dictionaries, and encyclopedias. He must be selective, using only those facts which suit his purpose.

Looking at history. Even if a writer does not want to use a historical approach, he can often get good ideas by looking at the history of his subject. Frequently, his mind is opened to new aspects of the topic.

Brainstorming

Brainstorming is a good way to see a topic from many points of view. A group of people can use all the methods described for gathering ideas except research, which would have to come later. Because each person has a unique background, a group can contribute many more ideas than one person can.

A brainstorming session is an excellent way to help a class see the scope of a topic and understand the use of different mental procedures for coming up with ideas. It is wise to establish certain ground rules, such as allowing time to record ideas, giving each student a chance to speak in turn, and avoiding criticism of any suggestion. To save time later in sharing results, a student with good handwriting and spelling should record ideas in columns on a ditto master as the teacher writes them on the chalkboard. Space should be left between columns as in the example that follows.

The word *red* is an excellent topic for brainstorming. Groups of seventh graders can think of as many as 125 words connected with red. Normally, students start with objects, and the teacher should remind them of procedures for coming up with other kinds of words. At least eight categories should be represented, and they should be offered in random order. Usually, the discussion takes forty or fifty minutes. The following day each student can be presented with a duplicated list of student words with lines drawn at intervals between the columns.

STUDENT BRAINSTORMING ON THE WORD *RED*

flowers _____	albino eyes _____
blood	freckles
stop	cars
crayon	tomato soup
paint	life savers
ink	thread
Mars	ketchup
apple	shoes
ribbon	lights
flag	dynamite
pens	yarn
dictionary	cardinal (bird)
cherry _____	Cardinals (team) _____
ambulance	Cardinal (R.C. leader)

fire engine
face
tomato
paper
glass
wine
shirt
strawberries
color _____
Redskins
second hand of clock
rose
geranium
label
socks
red writing in Bible
checkerboard
chaos
seeing red
red-nosed _____
Rudolph
Red Riding Hood
red snapper
encyclopedia
watch band
beware
Red Indians
valentine
Red Cross
red setter _____
robin
lipstick
rouge
sucker
food coloring
scab
wound
bloodshot eyes

sunset
heart
alarm
red barn
Red Baron
Redd Foxx
ruby
pink
sign _____
bar-b-q potato chips
Santa Claus
red-blooded American
ladybug
shoe laces
Red China
Pink Panther
votive light
Red Sea
crab
lobster _____
belt
hot tamale
Kool Aid
deck of cards
beets
diaper rash
toothpaste
fall colors
danger
war _____
hate
burgundy
maroon
orange
Reds and Pinkos
fire
sun
crimson

□ *How can ideas be organized for writing?*

After each student has seen the list of words, the big question is how to sort so many ideas for use in writing. Someone probably will quickly think of categorizing, but it is wise to allow discussion of other possible ways. There can be opportunities to review some ways of thinking introduced in previous chapters. For example, one student might suggest listing in alphabetical order; another student could be asked to point out why this would not work. A teacher needs to take time to encourage students who feel their way more slowly than others. The fact that they offer suggestions at all is promising.

Once the idea of ordering the words in categories has gained general acceptance, a discussion of possible category labels is necessary. A good ground rule is that there should be at least three items of a kind before a label is worth listing. Once again, *all* suggestions should be listed in columns. When a substantial number have been offered, possibilities of combining two or three can be mentioned. The use of arrows or brackets at this stage, rather than erasing, will demonstrate the mental process involved. When the class has come to an agreement, writing a neat final list will enable students to write labels on the lines provided between the words. This final list for *red* will probably include shades of red, red in nature, red objects, red clothes, red liquids, red food, red as a symbol, names using red, red used in religion, and expressions using the word *red.* After writing the category labels, students can choose at least three appropriate items from the word list and write them under each label. An example can be demonstrated with *Red Food.* It is best to choose things found in nature, like tomatoes, cherries, and lobsters, rather than listing ketchup, tomato soup, and suckers. It will take time and much practice for some students to learn how to make good selections. For the moment, the most important requirement is for an item to really belong to a category.

Individual student lists should be evaluated carefully. Students showing lack of understanding should receive help immediately, perhaps from a fellow student who has demonstrated competence in the area. It is insufficient to mark a list incorrect; students must have a clear grasp of category formation to be successful.

The logical ordering of categories should receive attention next. This will not be different in kind from the ordering of items within a category as shown in Chapter 5. One logical order for the *red* categories would be to move from most to least obvious. This order might take various forms: red objects, red clothes, red food, red liquids, shades of red, red in nature, names using the word red, red used in religion, red as symbol. On the other hand, red is primarily a color and is frequently present in nature, so these two categories could head the list.

Preparations can now proceed for the final exercise in forming paragraphs from categories before the writing of individual essays. Students can choose three of the *red* categories, place them in logical order, then check the items and their order. The title *red* goes at the top of the page, underlined, with a line left blank below it. The three indented topic sentences should be spaced on the page to allow for filling in the paragraphs. These topic sentences should be checked first; paragraphs can then be completed from the items. Correct form is the main aim, since this can be achieved by all students, and those who find writing easier can work on a smoother style. An elementary example follows.

RED

Many examples of red are seen in nature. Flowers are sometimes red. Even animals are occasionally red. Rubies are a kind of red stone.

Red comes in many shades from very light to very dark. Pink is often used for baby girls. Orange is easily seen and is sometimes used for uniforms or safety clothing. Burgundy is a very dark red.

Sometimes red is used as a symbol. When driving, we have to stop at a red light or red stop sign. A red flag shows danger. A red cross is a sign for medical help.

□ *What is the purpose of having an introduction and a conclusion?*

Learning how to put ideas together in an orderly way is the object of all the activities covered in these chapters. It is anticipated that a student who can put his own ideas in writing will have better reading comprehension. Since writers often use an introduction and a conclusion, the student should understand the purposes of these sections.

An excellent way to proceed with this discussion is to have students read a brief introduction and conclusion to a book or a chapter. They should be instructed to read these sections *only*. An opening question can be: "What do you know about this book or chapter from reading the introduction?" The same question can then be asked about the conclusion. Most students will probably be surprised to discover that they now know a considerable amount about the purpose and subject of the piece of writing.

Why are these sections desirable or even necessary? The writer wants to alert the reader to certain aspects of his material. The introduction may also be by another author who can establish the writer's credentials or introduce explanatory material. In the same way, the writer wants to help the reader at the conclusion of the material by summing up the main points or presenting his main idea in summary form. Both introduction and conclusion are designed to help the reader.

Writing an introduction

There is a procedure for writing a brief introduction. The writer can look upon his main title as a category label and use the category labels he has developed as items. Taking the *red* example, for instance, a topic sentence can be written based on the labels *red in nature, shades of red,* and *red used as symbol.* "There are several different aspects of *red.*" For some students, one sentence of this kind may be all they can manage at this point. Others can fill in a paragraph:

> There are several different aspects to *red.* It is an important color in nature. Red comes in many shades. As a symbol, it often represents danger or calls attention to help in emergencies.

Even a brief paragraph of this type serves the purpose of calling the reader's attention to the main points to be covered. At the same time, such a paragraph tells the reader that the writing will be descriptive rather than imaginative. The reader will know what *not* to expect.

Writing a conclusion

The procedure for writing a conclusion is not clear-cut and depends on the tone and style of the body of writing. Basically, it is a summing up and may incorporate material used in the introduction. An example of a simple conclusion might be the following:

> In conclusion, red is a word which means many things other than color to various individuals. It may be found in nature or be used to represent danger.

Having worked on an introduction and conclusion to *red* as a whole class, students should then work individually. The use of an impersonal, expository form will promote clear, practical reasoning and reduce student tendency to indulge in personal opinions. The subject used as an exercise can profitably be a topical one. Recent events in school or anticipated holidays may be more interesting and easier to understand than more academic subjects. Here is an example of a complete exercise built around a holiday.

WRITING INTRODUCTORY AND CONCLUDING STATEMENTS

Introduction

Introductory statements are used in conversation all the time. When we want to tell a friend about something that happened, we say things like: "Wait till I tell you what happened at the dance Friday!" or "Do you know what happened to me because I was late?" With this kind of remark, the speaker arouses the listener's interest and directs his attention to the subject. Just as we introduce conversation, we often conclude it with sentences like: "Believe me, I'll never do *that* again!" or "That was one of the best days ever!" These are comments about what has just been said.

Three paragraphs follow, each with a topic sentence. Space is left above the paragraphs to write a title and an introductory statement. There is room at the end for a conclusion.

Please do not write yet.

Directions. You are going to move parts of categories down one degree. The title will become a label; the labels will become items.

1. Read all three paragraphs.
2. Read each topic sentence. Make category labels. Write your label on the correct line where it says "Topic sentence _____ turned into *item* _____."
3. Write a label above the three items. (This label is really the title.)
4. Write a topic sentence based on your label. Read the label and the topic sentences over carefully to see whether they fit every single word of the three paragraphs. Write the label as your title.
5. When you have read the whole thing through, write a concluding statement. If you have trouble getting started, here are three suggestions for how to begin. "(subject) means . . . ," "In conclusion . . . ," and "We have seen that . . . ."

Making a category out of the title and three topic sentences

Title turned into the new *label* ___("The Christmas Season" is one possibility)___

Topic sentence 1. turned into *item 1.* ____(a busy time)____

Topic sentence 2. turned into *item 2.* ____(a religious event)____

Topic sentence 3. turned into *item 3.* ____(a time for fun)____

The text

(title) _____

(introduction)
(indent)   _____

_____

1.   It is a busy time of year. Crews are out hanging decorations in the main street. In spite of the cold, the streets are crowded with shoppers. Inside the houses, people are baking, sewing, writing cards, and wrapping gifts.

2.   To a few people Christmas is still mostly a religious event. It is a time to think about the birth of Jesus. There are special church services and concerts.

3.   For some people Christmas is a time for parties, presents, and good times. They think little of the religious meaning of Christmas. Just the same, people want to be friendly and be a part of the "Christmas spirit."

(conclusion)
(indent)   _____

_____

THE END

An exercise structured in this way gives students a system for arriving at a title and introductory statement. It also demonstrates shifting and recombining ideas within a hierarchy. For the teacher, this exercise is valuable as a means of diagnosing thinking problems. A few of these problems may be:

1. Incorrect labels made from topic sentences. If this is the case, three steps can be taken. Have the student read the sentences aloud to check on correct reading. Have the student give the meanings of the sentences in his own words. Have the student ask leading questions for the three sentences: "What kind of time is it?" "What does Christmas mean to a few people?" "What does Christmas mean for others?" The student needs practice asking these questions about other topic sentences in order to learn how to read them better.

2. Too broad a title, such as *Christmas*. The student should be asked to make a list of all the things he can think of associated with Christmas and then check to see how many items on his list are in the three paragraphs.

3. Too narrow a title, such as *Christmas Fun* or *Jesus' Birthday*. The student should be asked to write out all the items he can find in the three paragraphs and see if they will *all* fit under his title. (The analogy of an umbrella is sometimes helpful.)

A common thread running through all kinds of thinking problems connected with reading is that students may not stick to the text but go off on tangents of their own. Reading should set off trains of thought *after* a person learns to get the substance of a text. Such thinking problems may result from emotional immaturity and egocentrism or may be a sign of boredom with the subject. The more active the students become in making decisions about their reading, the less likely they are to be bored. Keeping assignments short and varying the approach is helpful.

Conclusion

Since the material covered in this chapter is so important to students for their individual writing, it might be helpful to duplicate a review sheet. This sheet, with the requirements of a good topic sentence studied in Chapter 5 and student sheets varying topic sentences suggested in Chapter 4, can become references for each student. Memorizing lists is probably not very valuable. If a student is having a problem, he can be referred to the relevant portion of the list and be asked to try again on his own. In this way, he will learn to go to his own references before asking for help. The following is a suggested review sheet.

HOW TO GATHER IDEAS FOR WRITING

Tapping personal experiences (Have you seen it? Travel, TV, books, magazines)

Finding associations of ideas (What does it remind you of?)

Using sense impressions (think of seeing, hearing, touching, tasting, smelling)

Using emotions (How does it make you or others feel? like, dislike, love, hate, anger, contentment, envy, fear)

Using symbols (Does it stand for something? Are special symbols connected with it? colors, flags, religious signs, signals, cars, clothing, words that are "loaded")

Using different meanings of words

Comparing and contrasting

Thinking about cause and effect

Doing research (finding facts, looking up history)

Brainstorming (thinking about the topic from all possible angles)

HOW TO USE THE IDEAS IN WRITING

Categorize the ideas

Choose the most important items for each category

Order the items logically (biggest to smallest, most to least important, chronological sequence, cause and effect)

Order the categories logically (most to least importance, familiar to unfamiliar, historical order)

Write topic sentences using the category labels (see sheet on formula)

Fill in the paragraphs with specific items in a logical order

Evaluation

Since there has been constant evaluation throughout the activities covered by this chapter and since the students will be making further use of everything for individual writing, a formal evaluation is not necessary at this point. Before starting individual writing, however, it might be a good plan to think about individual student strengths and weaknesses and the small groups of students needing special help. These groups may include two kinds of students: those who think clearly and independently but are deficient in writing skills and those who can write and spell but cannot think independently. Hopefully, with encouragement and praise for good thought processes, the first group will want to improve writing skills. The second group may need to review thought processes by going all the way back to the concrete image of the objects and labels and how they differed. The processes are basic and they must be understood before progress in reading comprehension can become possible.

CHAPTER EIGHT

Writing a Brief Essay

KEY VOCABULARY

brainstorming	process
categorizing	product
organizing	structure
logical ordering	system (-atic)
paragraph form	worksheets

KEY QUESTIONS

☐ Is a systematic approach to writing tasks possible?

☐ Why has a short essay been chosen as the form, or *product,* culminating the categorizing exercises?

☐ Why is it important to understand the *process* of gathering, organizing, and writing down ideas?

☐ Why will students get eight separate grades for completing the essay?

☐ Why is it important to keep all worksheets until the eight steps have been completed?

☐ Why is it important to follow paragraph form?

☐ Does learning a process for organizing ideas help people to read more intelligently?

Preview of possible answers

There is more than one way to go about a writing task, but each way must include the elements worked on in this project. It is useful to be thoroughly familiar with one approach before trying others. Anybody can produce a simple, clear piece of writing by using the method described here.

A short essay has been chosen for this project because it allows for personal choices and ideas, but it has a form similar to the one most commonly used in school texts and other formal writing.

It is important to understand the *process* of gathering, organizing, and writing down ideas so that it can be used in the future for any writing tasks. Students gain confidence in their ability to write if they know how to proceed with each assignment. This may encourage them to work on necessary skills.

The essay task is divided into eight separate assignments so that students can analyze difficulties and correct mistakes in each part of the process of writing. (The division also makes it possible for students lacking confidence to complete the essay since each step is a small one.) Each step needs to be discussed and evaluated. All worksheets should be kept for purposes of review.

Paragraphs are groups of ideas and have to be visually presented as such. The signal for a new paragraph is indentation. All the sentences must be joined to show their unity of purpose. Paragraph form conveys *meaning* and is therefore important.

Learning the process of organizing ideas will help students to understand the organization of other people's ideas when they read. The structure of the essay is a three-tiered hierarchy of title, labels, and items providing a framework for the sentences. Every set of directions and every poem, short story, or textbook read later has a framework or structure. Understanding these structures is basic to reading comprehension.

□ *Is a systematic approach to writing tasks possible?*

All writing tasks should be approached systematically, although the same system will not always be used. Careful preparation is absolutely essential for the success of the essay writing project. In the conclusion to Chapter 7, useful references for each student are mentioned: the requirements of a good topic sentence, student sheets with varied topic sentences to use as models, and a review sheet covering the gathering and using of ideas in writing. If each student has a folder for all his work, these references will be readily available. Students should be encouraged to use the references before asking for help.

The teacher must understand thoroughly the strengths and weaknesses of each student in order to anticipate the kind of help each may need. Even the slowest, least confident student is capable of completing a brief essay using the plan proposed; and he may need special individual help from a volunteer, teacher aide, or peer teacher. Informed and sympathetic school administrators may be encouraged to provide additional resource teachers for certain times. This additional help can also be used to supervise alternative work, either for groups not yet participating or for students waiting for help or having completed the essay. Since the students work individually on their essays, they complete assignments in widely varying amounts of time. Carefully planned alternative tasks are essential.

Alternative tasks can vary widely, according to the way in which the categorizing exercises are organized within the curriculum and depending on whether an entire class is writing the essay simultaneously. If content material, such as social studies, is available, students can immediately use it to practice some of the skills learned. For example, students can choose some category labels from the table of contents and list suitable items found in the material. Conversely, the teacher can give two items and set the task of finding a suitable label and additional items. Or he may present a label and items, requiring a paragraph to be built around them. Other applications can be devised from work with maps and graphs, such as listing under a suitable label all countries in Africa with a rainfall of less than 5 inches.

If the exercises are part of an English curriculum, similar tasks can be assigned. "Find the person who is described as tall, silent, male, and middle-aged in (name of story). Write down the name of this person, list the items under the name, and add any others you can find." Or, conversely, give the name of a character and ask for suitable items. Another approach would be to list characteristics such as height, weight, hair color, eye color, personality, and financial status and then ask students to fill in the information for characters in a story. Another possibility is to ask students to find the paragraph in which a person is described and to form a category from it. More creatively, the teacher can give students a name and some items (preferably humorous or exaggerated in some way) and ask them to write one or more paragraphs from the information.

☐ *Why has a short essay been chosen as the form,*
   or product, *culminating the categorizing exercises?*

A short essay allows for a formal structure, like a textbook, but also allows for considerable freedom of choice. A one-page essay is a reasonable task for both students and teachers and yet provides opportunities for careful attention to organization.

One teacher alone cannot handle a whole class for the essay project because of the need for rapid reinforcement throughout. In one trial, a classroom teacher and reading teacher together were able to conclude the essay project for a whole class in eight class sessions, but both spent an inordinate amount of outside time on evaluation. Careful student grouping, with two alternatives besides the essay, might enable a teacher to help one-third of the students with the essay at one time.

☐ *Why is it important to understand the* process *of gathering, organizing, and writing down ideas?*

Understanding the process of writing is essential to understanding how to read as well as write, since one is the reverse of the other. An analysis of process also allows teachers to find out at what point students are confused and it allows students to approach writing tasks in manageable steps.

A mental block needs to be mentioned. Most students do not seem familiar with the idea of working sheets, which sometimes look very messy. Teachers have often learned the dangers of discouraging student efforts with red marks all over the page, and they themselves are sometimes disturbed by untidy work. For learning, however, marks and remarks are essential. Prior discussion of this problem can go a long way toward reducing resentment. Teachers should, of course, guard against requiring spotless pages. Handwriting, spelling, and neatness are less important during the early stages than the thinking process of the student, and this fact is only visible with working sheets. All finished essays should be as beautiful as possible, hopefully duplicated and compiled into a booklet for others to read. Students will take a different attitude toward writing for a real purpose, such as providing reading material for another class.

Before a teacher decides that writing the essay is too large and bothersome a task, the alternative should be considered. It is ultimately more bother to cope with students making the same kinds of errors on all written work than it is to get to the bottom of the problem. The essay project is so arranged that a teacher can pinpoint types of errors for resource personnel, administrators, other teachers, and parents. By keeping all worksheets, a teacher can produce concrete evidence of his own systematic efforts and the needs of his students. For the teacher, an additional advantage in proceeding with the essay is that many students who have felt unable to cope with written tasks may find themselves able to complete this one, and this success may motivate them in other ways. Such students may begin to use previously untapped skills and intelligence.

☐ *Why will students get eight separate grades for completing the essay?*
☐ *Why is it important to keep all worksheets until the eight steps have been completed?*

Dividing the task of writing an essay into eight evaluated steps helps students to see where they are making mistakes. It also helps them to complete the work since each step is small, has already been demonstrated, and is carefully described. These steps are best revealed on the worksheets and, when the essay is complete, the worksheets can be used for reviewing the thinking processes and writing mechanics.

Teachers should provide each student with a copy of an essay checklist (see sample CHECKLIST FOR THE ESSAY). The sample list is based on the idea of giving eight separate grades for the work required. Lines provided in the left-hand margin are for the grades. This method breaks the tasks into small sections which can be accomplished by even the least gifted students. At the same time, all students become aware of the process of writing. From the teacher's point of view, an exact analysis of student thinking and writing problems is possible. Care should be taken to see that each student can read the checklist.

During the assignments, some problems requiring attention may become evident. Some students who easily convey meaning through conversation may have little ability for expressing ideas in writing. Lack of experience may result in inadequate concepts. Lack of organizational ability may hamper proper use of good ideas. Emotional immaturity may restrict a student to childish ideas which are narrowly self-centered. Lack of confidence may impede students from making use of their abilities. The teacher can make a real contribution by carefully evaluating each assignment while providing as much encouragement and support as possible. Suggestions made with a view to enabling students to succeed will normally be well received. Indiscriminate praise soon loses value; however, sincere praise for genuine effort can reward the gifted as well as the deprived student.

Each item on the checklist should be discussed with the class in order to make sure each student understands what is expected. The first item is most important. No grades should be given unless all worksheets are kept. It is helpful to staple each student's work together at the end of each work session, with the most recent work on top. (Each worksheet must have the student's name on it.) Students should be allowed to cross out neatly, draw arrows or other directional signs, and rework directly on the sheets. Through the changes made, the teacher can follow a student's thinking patterns.

Choosing a topic

The topics listed can be selected to suit a particular group of students, and they should be as open-ended as possible to allow room for a variety of categories. Some of the topics listed on the sample checklist are easier than others, and students who are likely to have problems should be gently steered toward an appropriate topic. If red is covered in class, it can serve as a model for *blue.* Symbolic use of blue is far less obvious than those symbols associated with *red*; however, many students know expressions like "I'm feeling blue," or they are familiar with songs about blue skies and can recognize music called "The Blues." *Spring* is another topic which produces ideas easily. Thinking of the several meanings of the word alone gives a series of categories. *Rock* also has a number of meanings and is used in many expressions familiar to students, such as "don't rock the boat," "on the rocks," "hitting rock bottom," and "rock" groups. Students choosing *sports* need to be alerted to the fact that the topic is not *Team Sports Played in Our School.* The wider topic should include sense impressions, emotions, and broad categories of a variety of sports. *War,* unfortunately, is usually topical, and some students watch television programs dealing with it. These students should be encouraged to think their way all around the topic, its consequences and effects, and not limit themselves to a discussion of hardware. *Night* is an excellent topic for imaginative children. *Fire, earth,* and *water* may have special kinds of appeal. The topic, *wheels* offers a broad scope, including historical development, industrial uses, feelings, and expressions like "wheeler-dealer," "he's a big wheel," and "the squeaking wheel gets the oil."

It is wise to have each student write one brief sentence stating why he chose a particular topic. A substantial reason should be given, rather than "I like it," although liking the topic is important. By writing a sentence, the student can focus more carefully on a topic instead of picking one at random.

Organizing ideas in categories

Success of the essay depends on careful organization of the list of ideas each student assembles into suitable categories. A good ground rule is to have at least three items in a category. If a student especially likes a category and does not have three items for it, he should receive encouragement to think of additional ideas. Rethinking the labels may allow inclusion of single items. Evaluating this part of the project is time-consuming because the teacher needs to get inside each student's frame of reference and judge the categorizing from that point of view. Eliminating whole categories without discussion is not helpful. The student may have a good idea which needs clarifying. All student ideas should be treated seriously.

While there can be great latitude in choosing categories, all students should grapple with some which are not concrete in nature. Such practice is important for training students to look at different aspects of a subject. The slow or immature student is quite capable of producing sense impressions and emotions associated with his topic. For future writing, for reading improvement, and for general mental development, all students should receive guidance that will expand their thinking beyond visible objects. It is helpful to students with limited ability to mention one item of a new category and have each student think of two others and a suitable label.

Three is not a magical number, but asking for three items in each category for the essay provides an ordering problem while reducing volume. All writers are forced to make choices and discard some good ideas. Students need to ask themselves how truly important to the topic an item may be. Sometimes, one item can represent several items, or a generic term may be used instead of a specific one. For example, in the *war* list a student may name six kinds of planes in a category labeled *planes,* while he might reduce the items by calling them transport planes, bombers, and fighters. In the *spring* essay, he might change a list of flowers to flowering bulbs, shrubs, and trees. These mental activities involve grouping within categories—a task that is essential in any short piece of writing.

☐ *Why is it important to follow paragraph form?*

When the paragraph writing begins, it is very important to insist that students indent the topic (or first sentence) and then write continuously. As the student creates a paragraph, he needs to be aware of its *form* in order to gain skill for future writing and reading tasks. The reader better understands that ideas belong together when they are physically linked and indented. Of course, other signals indicating separation are often used in print; but it is wise to impress one consistent way as students begin to learn to write. Presenting a short text without signals (indentation, captialization, and punctuation) is a convincing way of making students aware of the importance of signals. It is worth taking the time to make such a demonstration.

Some teachers may want to provide their students with a model essay, covering a topic other than those being used by the class. Instructive samples and an essay written by one twelve-year-old boy follow.

Sample 1
ON WRITING AN ESSAY

Writing an essay is a useful introduction to formal writing. This kind of writing is expected of students in school and in later writing of business or personal letters and reports.

The first problems are choosing a topic and gathering ideas. It is much easier to write about subjects which interest you, so it is wise to choose a subject you like. Techniques like remembering past experiences, using the association of ideas, thinking about emotions and sense impressions, and figuring out whether there are symbols connected with the chosen topic, can be used to gather more ideas.

Once ideas are collected, they can be sorted into categories. The essay will be more interesting if the ideas are varied; not all should deal with concrete objects. The category labels will show what each group of ideas has in common.

The order in which the categories are presented and the order of the items in those categories are important in helping the reader to understand and remember what he is reading. The order should be logical. Examples of this kind of order are: obvious ideas followed by less obvious ones; things happening often, followed by things happening seldom; large things followed by smaller ones; light shades moving to darker; near moving to far; or the reverse of any of these.

When the framework of categories and items is complete, writing can begin. It is very important to write a clear topic sentence to tell the reader what each paragraph is about. Once the topic sentence is written, items can be used for completing the paragraph. An introduction to the piece of writing may be useful for letting the reader know what to expect. A conclusion can sum up the main points of the essay.

Everyone can learn to write clearly although he may be unable to write beautifully and interestingly. Everyone also can learn to see more than one aspect of a topic or a person. Learning to see many sides of a subject and then to group ideas is very useful and can make life more interesting as well.

Writing an essay may not be easy for everyone, but the task goes more smoothly when thoughts are arranged in an orderly manner before the writing begins. Such order helps readers follow the thoughts and understand the author's meaning.

UMBRELLAS

Umbrellas are very useful objects. They can also be decorative.

Umbrellas have many different uses. They prevent people from getting wet when it rains. Without them the sun would sometimes get too hot. Outdoor restaurants use bright umbrellas to attract customers.

People buy umbrellas for different reasons. A chic young lady wants something elegant to complete her wardrobe. Older people want something practical to keep them dry. Golfers need huge, sturdy umbrellas in case they are caught in a shower.

Umbrellas have important parts. The part you see most is the material—often nylon, sometimes cotton or silk. The material stretches on metal ribs when the umbrella is open and is attached to tips on the ends of the ribs. People hold the object by a handle, plain or fancy, attached to a shaft of wood or metal with a sliding catch for opening and closing the umbrella.

Umbrellas have social uses. People meet by offering to share an umbrella in a sudden shower. It is easy to hide behind an umbrella to escape being seen by someone. On a crowded beach an umbrella can mark your location and help you find your things after a dip.

Umbrellas have some special symbolic and magical uses. Maharajahs and tribal chiefs have special umbrellas in royal colors held over them to let everybody know how important they are. A neatly furled umbrella became a symbol of surrender during World War II. Mary Poppins used a magic umbrella in order to appear and disappear.

Umbrellas reveal a great deal about their owners. They tell about their tastes, their attitudes, and perhaps how rich they are. At the same time, umbrellas are very practical objects.

An Essay Written by a
Twelve-Year-Old Boy

(For teacher information only)

NIGHT

There are many special things that happen at night.

Many astronomers look at the sky. They watch for changes in the stars. They watch for changes in the moon too. Astronomers study the stars in different constellations.

Different people have different emotions at night. Some get very scared at every little noise they hear. Some people are even so scared they don't leave the house. All people in urban areas keep their doors and windows locked so no one can enter.

Many people sleep at night. It is the only time of day for them to sleep. Many people are very tired and are happy to go to bed. Most people dream and some people snore. Little children look forward to the attention from their parents at bedtime.

There is a lot of violence in some places at night. Most people attack then because it is dark and they will not be seen. Many burglaries happen then too. If there was such a thing as vampires, they would be violent characters in the dark.

At night many things happen in nature. The sky turns dark because the sun has gone down. Different animals come out, like the bat and the owl. All turns to darkness and silence because of the few people out.

We have seen that "night" means a time of many wonderful and not so wonderful things.

Joe Sparacino

CHECKLIST FOR THE ESSAY

All worksheets must be handed in with the finished essay.
(Be sure your name is on each page.)

1. Choose one of the following titles as the subject of your essay or make arrangements to write about a title of your own choosing.

   blue sports rock war night spring wheels fire
                        earth   water

   Write down the title you have chosen and one sentence explaining why you have chosen it. ("I like it" is not a sufficient reason.)

2. Do your own brainstorming. At first, simply write on a sheet of paper everything that comes into your head. Read over your list. Did you include a *variety* of ideas? If you need more ideas, check your review sheet on ways to get ideas.

3. Organize your ideas into categories. There should be at least three items for each category. Underline each label and list the items correctly.

4. Choose the five most important categories, remembering to include some that are not objects. On a new sheet of paper, copy the five categories you have chosen, placing them in logical order. (You should be able to explain what kind of order it is.) Study the items in each category and decide which items are important enough to include in your essay. Place three of the items in logical order under each label.

5. Write the five category labels in logical order at least five lines apart in the margin of a new sheet of paper. After studying the items under that label, write a topic sentence for each label. REMEMBER TO INDENT.

6. In the margin below the label, copy the items selected for each category. Using these items, complete each paragraph, continuing the paragraph from the topic sentence. (The sentences should follow each other without any gaps.)

7. Reread your five paragraphs and make necessary corrections or adjustments. Now read the five labels and think of them as items for your title. Use the title and items for writing an *introduction*. (Paragraphs usually have more than one sentence.) Reread your introduction and the five paragraphs and write a conclusion or summary.

8. When your finished essay has been corrected, copy it as neatly as possible, remembering to keep each paragraph separate from the rest. *You should have seven indentations.*

☐ *Does learning a process for organizing ideas help people to read more intelligently?*

The activities throughout these chapters have been planned to teach the basic structure of ideas—the category. Categories have been translated into paragraphs and grouped in hierarchies. These, plus the writing of an essay, provide students with a framework for analyzing what they read.

The structure found in written material is all-important to comprehension. Certain conventions are used to convey this structure. The title, like a roof, covers everything that follows. The main sections, like different floors of a building, have variations in arrangement and detail but combine with other sections to form a solid piece of work. The unseen foundation on which the structure rests is the thinking that takes place before the writing begins. The experience of making a structure enables students to more easily find their way in materials written by others.

The different sections of a written work should be connected, much as the floors of a building are connected by a stairway. Transition passages often provide this connection in writing. Building such passages is difficult and comes best through long practice and much experience in writing and reading.

Students can improve their reading through writing even if their writing is elementary in nature. Few students aged twelve to fourteen are able to write a mature essay, but the effort of trying to put their own ideas on paper teaches them to think for themselves. Some essays naturally are much better than others, but all students make progress in thinking when they write their own.

It is important to find and explain mistakes in thinking. Ideas for teachers are provided in the short section of examples which follows.

EXAMPLES OF POSSIBLE ESSAY EVALUATION: FIRST FOUR TASKS

Teachers have found examples given here to be helpful. Each teacher, of course, will introduce a style of his own. The important teaching task is to take student work seriously.

Task 1. I have chosen *fire* as my topic because I like it.

Comment. Please tell me *why* you like it.

Rewrite: I have chosen *fire* as my topic because I live near a fire station and watch the engines coming and going.

Comment. Thanks, this is a good reason.

Task 2.
sirens
helmets
Smoky
helicopters
heat
smoke
flames
camp fires
firecrackers

Comment. These are all good ideas. You will have trouble making five categories with them. Here are a few words to suggest other categories:

red   crackling   lightning
    napalm   fear   water

Task 3.
Ways of Cooking
open fire
broiling
boiling
Things for Fires
sirens
fire trucks
hoses
ladders
Forest Fires
Smoky
helicopters
trees burning
rangers

Colors
red
yellow
blue
Weapons
napalm
flame throwers
burning houses

General Comment. This is a good start. Your topic sentences will be easier to write if you include the word "fire" in your labels. Example: *Ways of Using Fire for Cooking,* instead of *Ways of Cooking.* "Things" is never a good word. Are hoses any use without water?

Comment. Perhaps you could combine categories 2 and 3 to make room for another important kind of category. How about fire in nature, emotions connected with fire, sense impressions?

"Weapons" *are* important. Wouldn't *Ways of Using Fire in War* be a better label?

Task 4. *Ways of Fighting Fires*
hoses
water
trees burning

Comment. This is a good way of combining two categories. Is "trees burning" a *way* of fighting fires? Is it important to have both hoses and water? If you make changes, you can include other items?

Ways of Cooking with Fire
open campfire
under a broiler
on a grill

Comment. Good.

Sense Impressions of Fire
fear
choking on smoke
burning your fingers

Comment. How about pleasant sense impressions, like getting warm or watching flames? Is "fear" a sense impression or an emotion?

Colors of Fire
red
blue
yellow

Comment. Good.

Weapons Using Fire
napalm
flame throwers
burning down houses

Comment. Is "burning down houses" a weapon? You could change your label to *Ways of Using Fire in War,* or replace burning down houses with "fire bombs."

General comment. You are almost ready to go. What is the logical order of your categories? It is not clear to me.

Evaluation

The essay is a very important way of evaluating the success of the categorizing exercises. In addition, there are at least three other ways of evaluating the whole project before proceeding with the application and extension of skills learned.

The simplest test is to present four words, one of which is a label, and ask students to write a paragraph according to the scheme just used in the essay. For those who used the two forms of pretest suggested in Chapter 1, this is part of the posttest. Here is a sample as it can be presented to students:

Here are four words. Decide which one of them is the label, and then write a paragraph in the same way as for the essay.

owls   seagulls   birds   sparrows

Points to evaluate are 1) use of indentation, 2) use of the main idea to form the topic sentence, 3) fulfillment of requirements for structuring a topic sentence, 4) success in logical ordering of the items (in this case not very important), and 5) attention to writing about the unique feature of each item (bird of prey or night bird; water bird, living off fish and trash; small, common land bird, living on seeds and insects).

The second way of evaluating progress is to present students with a short text on or below grade level and ask them to identify the topic sentences. This procedure is the posttest in reading. Students need to be told that the topic sentence will not necessarily be the first one in the paragraph and that sometimes *no* topic sentence is used. Comparison should be made with points evaluated in the pretest (see Chapter 1). The written material should not be difficult and could be taped for poor readers. Decoding is not the main object here. A sample is given for demonstration purposes.

Sample Paragraphs for Evaluation

(Underlining indicates topic sentences and
should be omitted when the material is presented.)

TIMBER ELEPHANTS

Care of Timber
Elephants
mahout
bath
salt
not too much work

Elephants that work with timber are well cared for. Their mahouts give them baths every day, rubbing their hides with rough bark or coconut husks. They are given extra salt and favorite fruits. Work is limited to three or four hours a day a few days a week, never when it is very hot.

Stages of Growth
light work at 16
fully grown at 25
too old to work
 at 65
die at 75 or earlier

Young elephants start doing light work at sixteen years-of-age. At twenty-five they are fully grown and ready for heavier work. At sixty-five they have trouble working. They usually die before they are seventy-five. Stages of growth in elephants are similar to those of humans.

Timber elephants do not have senses as keen as wild elephants. They have nothing to fear, so there is no reason to be alert. [Either sentence (or none) can be considered a topic sentence.]

[The first sentence is not really a topic sentence.]

Male elephants often have tusks, but the strongest males have none. In a fight, a tuskless elephant can wind his trunk around his enemy's tusks and throw him or break the tusks. Male Indian elephants often stand eight or nine feet tall and weigh about five tons.

Work elephants do	Elephants are especially useful in the
drag logs	forests because they are strong and can move
break up log jams	around easily. They drag logs to streams or
	roads where men collect them.
	Sometimes a slide is built down to a stream and
	the logs slide down it into the water. If
	there is a log jam, elephants can
	get into the stream to break up the jumble.

Another excellent measure of acquired skills can be derived from recently covered reading material by presenting familiar subject matter as "empty" categories and asking students to predict items without recourse to reading. A title, introductory statement, and four or five labels should be included. At least one label should clearly require a specific order for the items. When the assignment is completed, students can compare their items with those in the text. Items which differ are not necessarily wrong, but they should be checked by the teacher.

Selections of items to go with a topic sentence or topic sentences to fit items within a text can provide other possible reading exercises. The former requires identification of specific ideas while the latter requires ability to generalize or recognize general statements.

The final test can cover the categorizing process; and there are indications that understanding this process helps students transfer skills to other areas. Evaluating student knowledge of the process may, at the very least, help to indicate strengths and weaknesses. There are many ways in which this evaluation could be done. A sample written test appears on the opposite page.

Conclusion

Most students should show a marked improvement on the tasks evaluated. This should be the signal then to begin immediate application of the acquired skills to other learning tasks, especially reading. Chapter 9 introduces other suggestions for improving reading.

In the case of the few students who show little or no improvement, a review of their work should lead to discovery of exactly what problems they have. A complete review in a small group, starting with the categorizing of objects, may be very helpful. Some students simply need more time than others. Learning disabilities of various kinds hamper them, and careful observation may reveal some problems.

CATEGORIZING TEST

1. Putting objects, ideas, or events into groups and labeling them is called __(categorizing).__

2. In order to sort items into groups, we look for the __(common characteristics)__ of the items.

3. When we have decided what all the items share, we use this information to think up a __(label)__ for the group of items.

4. A category is made up of a __(label)__ and a group of __(items).__

5. When we write, we can use a category to build a __(paragraph).__

6. When we use a category to build a group of sentences, we use the label to write the __(topic)__ sentence.

7. We use categorizing for survival, for learning and remembering, and for problem solving. Using categorizing helps you to do tasks well and quickly, a result called being __(efficient).__

8. We learn from experience, from sense impressions, and from categorizing. These things help us to __(predict)__ what will happen.

9. What is the next number in this series: 2, 4, 8, 16 __(32)__? Write a good label for this group of numbers: __(Series of even numbers, each doubled, starting with 2).__

10. Add two words to this group: red, yellow, blue __(green, purple).__ Write a label for the group: __(Colors).__

11. Give three examples of the category, __States of the U.S.:__ __(Maryland)__, __(Oregon)__, __(Texas)__.

Put the following items from the original list in all possible squares:
birthday candle
notebook
raincap

color	Blue	White	Multicolored
function	Clothing	Writing material	Power source
form or structure	Number	Rectangular flat	Folded triangle
material	Paper	Plastic	Wax

Applying the Categorizing Process to Reading: Building Additional Thinking Skills

KEY VOCABULARY

facts	negative statements
information	conditional statements
opinions	alternation statements
main ideas	cause and effect
infer - inference - inferring	reasons - reasonable
imply - implied - implication	propaganda
connote - connotation	advertising
clues	relationships
drawing conclusions	functional (abstract) words

KEY QUESTIONS

☐ How can the previously described system of collecting and organizing ideas be used to understand how writers have organized their ideas?

☐ What reinforcement activities are essential in order to assure retention and use of this system for both reading and writing?

☐ Can other aspects of language development and usage be incorporated into this system as aids to better reading and writing?

☐ Can students derive other systems of organization from a thorough understanding of how categories are built and used in reading and writing?

Preview of Possible Answers

Being able to perform a task or having attempted it helps people understand and appreciate the way others do it. This is true of activities in sports, the arts, and mechanics, as well as in reading and writing. Preceding chapters explain ways for students to collect and organize their own ideas; and demonstrations are provided on assembling categories and building paragraphs around them, placing these paragraphs in logical order, and writing a short piece on different aspects of a chosen topic. Using this process in reverse will aid reading comprehension. For instance, the student identifies sections of a given piece of writing: introduction, conclusion, unit, chapter, and paragraph. He seeks the main ideas or labels, and the facts or items, and relates the parts to the whole.

Learning of lasting significance may occur in a flash when all necessary components have been assimilated beforehand. More often, time and repeated practice are necessary. In either case, the learning will not really be useful until it is absorbed into the student's own system of concepts, a process which usually takes many exposures.

Experience has demonstrated that one-shot teaching has little value. Everyone understands this when it comes to learning practical skills. Teaching of physical coordination is carefully planned to allow plenty of practice of each phase of a particular skill. The separate skills are then combined in an actual total operation. This fact has to be kept firmly in mind when isolating any part of a written statement for purposes of emphasis and analysis. The separation must be temporary only.

Mental coordination requires the same systematic instruction and practice as physical coordination. Once the task has been learned in its entirety, its application in "real" situations is essential. These applications involve thinking, writing, and reading activities of different kinds and should use classroom content or genuine student interests as subject matter. Identifying groups of ideas, fitting items into appropriate categories, finding or constructing labels for groups of items, and logically ordering categories and items within them are appropriate activities with any subject matter.

A firm foundation of categorizing ability (using language to name labels, to list items, and to build paragraphs around these structures) can furnish a systematic procedure for studying other aspects of language development and usage. Students can learn ways of combining sentences for style improvement and economy. Different kinds of sentences can be evolved to fit different thinking patterns. The proper use of certain function words in writing and the recognition of their function in reading are other essential elements. Students can study the implications of language, and they can ferret out various clues to hidden meaning. All activities using language can contribute to a better understanding of written material.

Other systems of organization can be added to the one simple categorizing process studied so far. Students can learn to write and recognize paragraphs which include topic sentences in different positions or paragraphs which have no topic sentence. Some other organizational patterns within paragraphs are: cause and effect statements, conditional statements, statements about a choice, negative statements, and comparisons. Examples of all these patterns can be found in textbook material. From what is known of the learning process, there is little question that these patterns are best introduced through the students' own ideas. How this is worked into the curriculum will depend on the age level and mental ability of the students and on the type of content being studied. The later reading models should be worthwhile in themselves, rather than isolated snippets demonstrating a particular technique. Some students can produce models for others. Thinking, reading, and writing should be coordinated so that the student can feel he is gaining competence in a content area while learning different techniques.

Too often, adults assume simplistic relationships in what are really very complex learning tasks. Teachers and curriculum specialists need to analyze the *thinking* tools necessary for reading specific assignments and to arm students with these tools prior to analysis of printed matter.

Thinking, listening, and speaking create the backbone of communication and, hence, of reading and writing. Most activities suggested in this book start with some listening and speaking, even if that fact is not being stressed. Sharpening these tools is a necessary prerequisite to improving reading and writing.

The various purposes and styles of written material can emerge gradually from and through student writing. Development of these skills depends somewhat on the student's maturity and need, as well as on his repeated exposure.

On occasion, schools receive criticism for stifling creativity. In the approach presented in this volume, there is no intent to belittle creative impulses. Learning to handle the tools of a craft does not prevent a person from producing an individual product. On the contrary, mastering technical skills frees students to express themselves. Creativity does not mean an absence of discipline but rather sufficient discipline to learn skills and move beyond them. Making the skills an end in themselves may indeed stifle creativity and learning. Skills utilized in meaningful activities confirm in students their worth. Learning to see many sides of a topic expands students' horizons and helps them to develop wider perspectives. Once a person has dealt with a topic in breadth, he can work in depth on a small, highly personal aspect. Students can practice different ways of expressing their feelings appropriately, including free, associative writing. They will do this only if their ideas and feelings are valued and their privacy is protected. In summary, learning to build and use categories will not hamper personal expression unless teachers impose their own ways of seeing things on the students instead of helping them to develop their own views and supporting them when they take risks. Encouraging many different modes of communicating helps to prevent rigidity.

This chapter advocates that teachers constantly refer to the students' own concepts when teaching techniques of reading and writing. Although this procedure may seem wearisome, it will save time in the long run, make it possible for many more students to make progress, and increase chances of student mental growth. The techniques should first be used consciously with old ideas, then immediately applied to other ideas related to subject matter under study or to the students' daily lives. This application most often consists of reading, which involves a reversal of the procedure used for writing. As mentioned in the preface, this is an extension of the language experience approach.

Space limitations make it impossible to provide examples from textbooks and literature to suit every situation. Classroom teachers, reading teachers, and curriculum specialists can find relevant, available materials. They know the curriculum, the student levels, and the community expectations. It is hoped that the thinking tasks presented here are explained clearly enough to facilitate the finding of suitable reading material. The whole approach advocated in this book is intended for the many teachers who want to understand their students' problems and find ways to assist them. Ingredients are listed, but the precise recipe has to be left to the good sense and creativity of classroom teachers.

Introduction

A few introductory remarks need to be made before plunging into the specific suggestions for using previously learned procedures as aids to reading comprehension and additional thinking skills. The suggestions do not supplant, but complement, approaches advocated in standard texts which provide teaching strategies for reading instruction.

A plea must be made at the outset that all students be given time and a friendly atmosphere in which to do independent reading. The best reading instruction cannot substitute for *pleasure* in reading. Without pleasure, students will not acquire a lifelong reading habit, which is the ultimate goal. The best way to stimulate plea-sure and motivation is to encourage all reading interests in all mate-rial. If "trash" reading provides enjoyment of reading, eventually better reading will follow as the students mature and improve their reading skills through practice. Most students find material that they can enjoy. The reading teacher can supply additional materials, selecting the better comic books and illustrated materials on sports, racing, mechanics, and other popular topics. Schoolwide reading can be excellent when the administration and staff back the idea and take part. The technicalities require careful planning, implemen-tion, and constant evaluation.

This chapter makes suggestions for enlarging students' thinking and reading skills. None of the suggestions can succeed as one-shot teaching techniques; they need careful incorporation into the curriculum and regular use in different contexts over a period of time.

The procedure advocated in this chapter, as in the others, is to start with thinking skills students use in their daily lives. A particu-lar process is isolated, looked at from different angles, manipulated in some way, then applied to reading. Most of the skills discussed in this chapter can be applied to every page the students read in any book.

One may rightly ask, "Why is it that students have problems reading passages containing logical inferences they use daily?" Daily use relies to a large extent on known formulas, and the sentences are always within a familiar context. Both concepts and vocabulary may be unfamiliar in reading.

While we should never underestimate a student, we should nevertheless take neither mental processes nor information for granted. Simple prelesson acitivities can prevent frustration for teachers and students alike. A brief review of fundamentals done in a matter-of-fact way with student participation insults no one. The atmosphere in the classroom should be stimulating and businesslike, without being threatening.

Some teachers may say, "This is all very well, but I have students who cannot read the *words*. Let the reading teacher teach them to read the words." Students who pose these tremendous problems to the teacher may develop into worse individual problems when they are removed from the classroom for extended periods. They may have had heavy doses of phonics instruction which were ineffective for one reason or another. These students may be helped through the approach of relating each part of learning to their lives and to the classroom content material, of having diverse activities which involve skills other than reading, and of creating a situation where students are encouraged to be helpful to each other. Sometimes working backwards, from meaning and involvement with concepts to phonics, is very effective, especially with older students. Phonics and spelling can be learned with the basic vocabulary of the subject under study, just as well as from packaged materials. The student then has a reason to learn since it enables him to participate in classroom activities. A few small successes and some moral support can transform apparently hopeless cases.

Some teachers may consider the student writing advocated in this chapter to be an intolerable burden. Studies have shown, however, that it is not necessary for teachers to evaluate every piece of writing. Students can evaluate each other's work according to agreed criteria. Small groups of five or six students get together to complete a particular task: each group has a chosen leader and a secretary; they have a check sheet; they discuss and understand the purpose of the activity as well as the details of the check sheet. Students who experience great technical difficulties in writing and spelling should be placed in groups with able students who can assist them; they should not be segregated into remedial groups because they may be unable to function and, consequently, will become disruptive. Each group completes the task, shares papers, fills out the check sheet, and staples student papers to it. Each student needs only one piece of paper, even if an assignment has to be corrected and rewritten. The teacher needs to see what has taken place. A neat line through the first draft will show that evaluation should be based on the next version. The class then gathers for a reporting session and the reading of models or discussion of data on the check sheet. The teacher grades on the basis of the check sheet, class discussion, and a posttest item such as another version of the task. Organization then, is the key to success for this method which has worked well in junior high open-space classes of up to 120 students and in traditional classes of up to 35 students. Certainly, the procedure requires more work of teachers *before* the activity, but it allows a great deal of student writing without creating mountains of papers to be corrected. The sample check sheet illustrates.

The procedures discussed here are intended to help students become independent readers. A problem for those moving up from elementary schools where the emphasis has often been on word reading is that they feel guilty if they skip words. When students are asked to read textbooks without being shown how to

CHECK SHEET FOR THE STYLE CHANGING ACTIVITY

(Use the back of this sheet if necessary.)

Class period _____ Date _____ Student leader _____
Secretary _____
(substitute leader)

Check "style" paragraphs worked on: Nos. 1. ____ 2. ____ 3. ____
4. ____

Students in the group   *Evaluation* Group evaluation = G.E.
Self evaluation = S.E.

_____	G.E. 1.____ 2.____ 3.____ 4.____
	S.E. 1.____ 2.____ 3.____ 4.____
_____	G.E. 1.____ 2.____ 3.____ 4.____
	S.E. 1.____ 2.____ 3.____ 4.____
_____	G.E. 1.____ 2.____ 3.____ 4.____
	S.E. 1.____ 2.____ 3.____ 4.____
_____	G.E. 1.____ 2.____ 3.____ 4.____
	S.E. 1.____ 2.____ 3.____ 4.____
_____	G.E. 1.____ 2.____ 3.____ 4.____
	S.E. 1.____ 2.____ 3.____ 4.____
_____	G.E. 1.____ 2.____ 3.____ 4.____
	S.E. 1.____ 2.____ 3.____ 4.____

Criteria for evaluation

1. Has the paragraph been noticeably changed?
2. List key words or phrases used in the second version of the paragraphs by any student.

    Para. 1. *Label* _____
    Words _____
    _____

    Para. 2. *Label* _____
    Words _____
    _____

    Para. 3. *Label* _____
    Words _____
    _____

    Para. 4. *Label* _____
    Words _____
    _____

3. Have all corrections been made and a clean version written?
4. Has sentence structure been altered? ____ In what way? (shorter, longer, more complex, less complex)

    Para. 1. _____
    Para. 2. _____
    Para. 3. _____
    Para. 4. _____

skim for pertinent information, they often develop a dislike of reading. In this chapter, the emphasis will be on the structure of reading material. Being able to find the basic structure of a reading passage helps students to skim intelligently, as long as they are encouraged to do so. Acquisition of this skill is especially important for poor readers, making it possible for them to cover the main points even if they cannot finish all the reading. Every reading assignment should be carefully designed to include prior discussion, to establish one or two specific purposes for reading, and to provide review afterwards.

☐ *How can the previously described system of collecting and organizing ideas be used to understand how other writers have organized their ideas?*

Once translating letters into sounds (decoding) has been mastered, reading is essentially the reverse of the mental process used for writing. In both cases, one-way communication is being attempted. There is no dialogue and no intermediary person using gestures and facial expressions or answering questions for clarification.

The writing process ends with the finished statement. Reading begins with this satement, and the reader must consciously or unconsciously work his way back to the original structure in the writer's mind and to his purpose for making the statement.

What are some questions a reader must ask in order to unravel the chain of thought? (Not all questions will be asked for each reading experience.)

1. Is there an introduction stating the writer's point of view, purpose, and perhaps his intended audience?
    Is the writer trying to see all sides of the topic, writing in a purely personal way, or is he seeking to influence the reader in a certain direction?

2. What is the date of publication?
    What are the author's qualifications if he is writing as an authority on the subject?

3. What is revealed about the organization of ideas on the printed page by the signals: size of typeface, colors used on the printed page, spacing, indentation, punctuation?

4. Are statements (topic sentences) followed by illuminating details, examples, reasons, or proofs (items)?

5. Are statements and items presented in a logical order and, if so, what is that order?

6. Is there a conclusion or summary?

7. What is the tone or style of the whole statement: informative, polemic, humorous, emotional, pompous, flowery? What key words indicate this tone? Are sentences short and direct or long and involved?

8. Are implications hidden "between the lines"? What words or phrases indicate these?

9. If people, places, or situations are described, does the description enable the reader to visualize the scene? Which words or phrases relate to sense impressions?

Previewing for reading

1. The writer's point of view

   Purpose. The writer's point of view, purpose, and intended audience determine his way of writing. Advance notice of these helps the reader to prepare his mind, decide whether he wants to proceed, and know what particular bias to watch for. Accounts of an accident can be quite different as given by drivers, witnesses, and a policeman. Disputes at school are described differently by student participants, onlookers, and teachers. A person's statement is influenced by his interests in a matter (revenge, fear of punishment, enforcement of discipline) and his way of looking at life. The style of a statement depends on the audience. Are we telling friends or the principal about an incident? Student skits can illustrate the effect of purpose on statements made about an episode.
   A good way to start a discussion of application of this knowledge to reading might be with a demonstration, perhaps as a learning station or small-group activity, of widely different pieces of writing: a book for young children, a long advertisement (see daily junk mail), two or three textbooks on different subjects for different levels of students (borrowed from colleagues), an advanced technical book, and a paperback gothic novel with a picture and blurb on the cover. If there is a local or national election coming up, political statements might be added. It is by no means necessary for students to be able to read these materials in their entirety; they need only establish whether the author reveals his point of view, purpose, and intended audience and, if so, what they are.

Attitude. A corollary to identifying purpose is the question, "How does the author handle his material?" Is he trying to present all sides of the question, reveal his own experience, or influence the reader in a particular way?

2. Facts the reader needs to know

Date of publication. The date of publication is of major importance in some types of factual reading. This importance can be demonstrated by asking students to find the facts on a particular page of an old textbook on science or social science. Even the least informed student may be astonished to read that we are dreaming of flying to the moon or breaking the sound barrier "some day," or that most of Africa consists of colonial territories. Students learn, in addition, that they cannot always believe everything they read just because it is in print.

Qualifications of the author. If the reading is supposed to be informative, the qualifications of the author can be very important. A librarian may aid in the illustration of qualified reporting by providing several writings at different levels on a topic under study. Students can evaluate the usefulness of these for their own purposes and those of college students.

3. Organization of ideas on the page

Teachers may be astonished to discover that most students do not *see* all of the helpful signals printed on a page. Even the more recent school materials, often beautifully organized, are not really *seen*. Why is this? Many students think that reading means deciphering individual words, and they are so preoccupied with this task that they do not even look for helpful hints about meaning. The individual words would seem much easier if all signals were clearly understood. Repeated exercises are useful in training students to look for signals (see the sample check sheet on reading signals).

Punctuation is usually taught as a writing activity, often accompanied by a set of rules, with inadequate explanation that the purpose of punctuation is to guide the reader. Punctuation is a set of signals meant to trigger mental activities. This concept is perhaps lost because students do a great deal of writing without any expectation of having it read by anyone other than the teacher, and "He will know what I mean."

CHECK SHEET ON READING SIGNALS: PREVIEWING A PAGE

Title of book _____ Student _____
_____ Period _____ Date _____

Page No. _____

1. What is the main heading or title on this page? _____
   _____

2. How do you know this is the main heading? (Place a check (√) to
   indicate answers.)
   Larger print _____ Different shape of letters _____
   Large amount of space around heading _____
   Different colored print _____ Different colored background _____
   Other ways (state) _____

3. What other headings or subheadings are on this page?
   _____
   _____

4. How many paragraphs are there? _____
   What signal is used to mark the beginning of each paragraph?
   _____

5. How many colors do you see on this page? _____

6. What illustrations, drawings, diagrams, or items in boxes are there?
   (Write in the title given, or write one yourself.)
   _____
   _____
   _____

7. How many question marks can you find? _____

There is a direct analogy between punctuation and traffic
signals. Everyone understands that action is required by traffic
signals. In reading, physical actions can stand symbolically for mental actions. A student can be asked to start walking when he sees the
capital letter, to pause briefly for every comma, and to stop for a
period. The question mark requires raised eyebrows. A comma,
unless it separates items in a list, tells the reader that there is more
than one thought in the sentence.

Special attention needs to be paid to quotation marks. The
most vivid way of showing what action is required by quotation
marks is to read a dialogue aloud with a proper cast of characters and
a narrator, while other students follow in the book. The characters
should stand in such a way as to make it clear who is talking to whom,
the crucial question. Every student should practice doing this, having had a chance to read over his part first.

Another misunderstood type of signal is the numbering and lettering used to order a sequence of ideas. The important aspect of these signals is not so much the particular hierarchy of numbers and letters but the fact that consecutive numbers and letters indicate that all the ideas belong to one category under the same label. Relationship to the margin then indicates the importance of the group of ideas in the hierarchy.

4. Looking at the conclusion

From Chapter 7 activities, students may remember that looking at the conclusion often helps readers focus on the main points of a piece of writing. Asking for one or two important ideas in a few conclusions is enough to help students realize that the kind of summing up often done at the end of chapters, units, or books can save them time in reading.

Reading for meaning

1. Type of item used in paragraphs with topic sentences

This information can be given about a portion of writing, preferably one or two paragraphs. The easiest way to get a clear picture is to translate the paragraph(s) into a category. Items can then be described: descriptive details, examples, proofs or reasons, or other types. If the paragraphs are wisely chosen, students will become aware that there are different ways of using paragraphs. Suggestions later in this chapter will explain this further.

2. The logical order in which ideas are presented

This information would again have to be given for a limited number of paragraphs. In a social studies text the order may be chronological or thematic; in a novel or scene or person may be described or an event described chronologically. In each case, there should be a reason for presenting ideas in that particular order. There is no need to belabor the point; just help students to keep order in mind as one part of organization, one way of conveying meaning.

3. The tone or style

The style of a piece of writing alerts a good reader to the intentions or limitations of an author. Being aware of the kinds of words and sentence structure that create the style is one aspect of becoming a competent reader. Such awareness is largely a matter of reading experience and maturity; it cannot be rushed but has to be developed gradually over a long period. Certain initial exercises, however, can help students understand what is involved.

The discussion can begin with an analogy which all students can understand. Style in language, spoken or written, is like clothing. All of us wear different clothes for different occasions and talk to different people in different ways; this can best be illustrated by prepared group skits. Each group should plan a skit around a particular situation and wear suitable clothing when presenting the skit. The groups who watch should evaluate both the language and costumes for suitability to the occasion. Students can develop imaginative skits from their memories of old television programs and movies. Skits covering student experiences such as an interview with a principal, the organization of a party for friends, an attendance at a wedding or a funeral, a back-to-school-night scene, or the participation in a field trip can promote understanding of style.

Televised programs are now of such variety and frequency that they may be one of the richest resources for showing contrasts in style. Students can imitate characters, write a short dialogue of a scene from memory, list key words heard, describe or draw a picture of one of the characters, or show in some other way that they have understood the elements of a style. At this stage, demonstrating a *feeling* for style is more important than listing the elements. (Many poor readers are good actors and mimics; and activities of the type described can allow these students to excel in class, which in turn adds to their self-esteem and contributes to their learning.)

The most obvious elements of written style are vocabulary and sentence length or structure. Just reading and commenting on different styles will probably not help students to understand real differences. Asking them to write immediately in different styles may prove too difficult, although it is a future goal. For the moment a combined approach may be the answer.

Using the check sheet provided in the introduction, groups of students can work together on changing the style of brief reading passages. This practice can be entertaining as well as instructive if the initial material is brief and carefully chosen. Exaggerated examples are most effective to begin with. Here are two examples:

1. *Emotional*   Mary flung herself down by John's mangled body and wept hysterically, while the crowd of sensation-

seekers pushed and shoved. Rescue workers desperately tried to reach the victim and had to use their fists and elbows to get through the crowd.

Factual   Mary knelt beside John, who had been severely injured by the fall. She was not in control of herself. A large crowd gathered. Rescue workers had to use force to reach the injured man.

2. *Factual*   The band concert was at seven o'clock in front of the memorial. The red and gold uniforms looked fine in the fading sunlight. The crowd especially enjoyed the "Battle Hymn of the Republic."

Effusive   The long-awaited band concert finally took place at seven o'clock in front of the memorial to heroes of days gone by. The red and gold uniforms reflected the glorious hues of the sunlight. The enthusiastic crowd went wild over the stirring strains of the "Battle Hymn of the Republic."

Comparison of one or two examples done by the whole class may help students to understand the task.

Emotional Statements	*Factual Statements*
flung herself down	knelt
mangled body	severely injured
wept hysterically	not in control of herself
desperately	. . . . . .
victim	injured man

Comparison of sentence structure can follow the same sequence of group discussions.

As groups complete the tasks, each can report group results to the whole class. A master list of certain kinds of words can be compiled under appropriate headings. Student challenges should be encouraged. It may be helpful to point out clichés and phrases that are pompous, effusive, or humorous. Inexperienced readers do not necessarily recognize clichés and may even believe thay have discovered a great new way of saying something.

A variation of the task might be the recording of two versions of a television program such as a soap opera, a hospital or medical story, or a family program like *The Waltons.* The two versions would be 1) a strictly factual account of actual events and 2) a highly emotional or excessively sentimental description. Students might develop a dialogue to be performed in class. They could then follow the same procedure for "tough guy" programs.

After writing paragraphs in different styles, the time is ripe for observing how various authors create style. Again, the amount to be read should be limited to avoid discouraging students. Those who are avid readers will undoubtedly do additonal reading, and their example may stimulate others. English teachers will have no problems finding good examples in anthologies: Mark Twain, Edgar Allen Poe, and William Saroyan immediately come to mind. Social studies classes may study the different styles used in newspapers: news items, advertisements, editorials, and letters to the editor. Controversial writers in history, such as Jonathan Swift or Thomas Paine, offer other possibilities.

4. Implications hidden "between the lines" and the words or phrases serving as clues

Implications, connotations, and inferences are difficult and subtle elements of reading comprehension. The vocabulary used to describe hidden meaning is itself difficult for many students to interpret. A listing on the chalkboard under a good label, perhaps *Words Describing Hidden Meanings,* should help in identifying the terms. The temptation to skip this step in favor of spending extra time on "functional" reading should be resisted because all citizens need to be on guard against false claims, whether political or commercial. The ability to separate fact from fiction or opinion is an essential part of reading comprehension and can help people avoid serious errors. Using imagination or visualizing, detecting hidden meanings, and noting omissions are vital to functional reading.

Within the school, teachers can easily collect examples of statements with hidden meanings which are familiar to all students. Sarcasm is an obvious example. The gym teacher, observing listless students doing push-ups, says, "Please don't strain yourselves." In announcing a test, the teacher says, "Now I know you all love tests." Other hidden meanings are revealed through statements such as, "Mrs. Z. is okay (pause) for a teacher," "Not bad tennis, for a girl," or "The movie is trash, but the kids will like it."

After class discussion of school examples of hidden meanings, students can collect advertisements (television, magazine, or newspaper) and write brief sentences showing the implications within each advertisement. For example, a cigarette advertisement shows a glamorous couple in a romantic setting. This is analyzed as "People who smoke Brand X are glamorous." Once students have analyzed a number of advertisements, they can organize them in certain categories. While there are excellent materials available on propaganda techniques, allowing students to work out their own categories, even if less complete, will help them to think the matter through. The exact labels do not matter, provided they express the right meaning.

Another useful and entertaining exercise is to have groups write examples of conversations, advertisements, or statements with hidden meanings and act them out for the class. Individual listeners can write one-sentence expressions of what the hidden meaning is and then compare collected ideas. Groups should receive guidance in thinking about the intended audience, the purpose of the statement or dialogue, and the consequent style to be used.

Another important aspect of hidden meanings is the power they may have over the emotions so that important facts will be ignored. Any advertisement should give customers information about total price, availability, and durability. Any political statement should explain how programs will be financed or which programs will be cut. A reader or listener should be able to make categories from the statements labeled *Why I Should Buy Brand X* or *Why I Should Vote for Y*. The items should answer the questions, How much? How many? How long? Who? What? When? Where? This procedure can be tried with advertisements and other statements which seek to persuade. If the statements do not answer the questions, they are likely to be opinions or irrelevant ideas. Students can seek real answers to the questions in the local store, from the manufacturer, or in a consumer's guide. They can make a collection of objects and display them with their advertisements and completed categories entitled *Facts About X*. This is functional reading and writing.

*5. Descriptions of people, places, or situations
that enable the reader to visualize the scene*

While television may have enlarged our horizons, most viewers have little opportunity for exercising imagination. Intelligent reading requires imagination. Simple directions become very difficult to follow when the reader cannot visualize various elements and their relationships. A true reader can visualize characters, a scene, or an approaching threat within a story. In this process the picture from the author's mind is transferred to the reader's mind—the whole object of writing and reading. If there is no picture, or an incomplete picture, there is little meaning. If there is little meaning, little of the content will be remembered. Perhaps students often choose to read a book after they see a screen version because they have already "received" the pictures which go with the words. Reading then becomes an act of recall rather than re-creation of the author's intention.

A good test of both observation and the ability to visualize a scene is to ask students to write a brief description of a very familiar home scene (father, mother, or well-known person cooking breakfast or dinner). The description should include the approximate size of the room (as compared to the classroom perhaps), the furniture (color and material), facts about people (size, shape, relationship to others), and references to odors, textures, and light conditions. Having written this in class without prior warning, the student can rewrite the piece at home, correcting and filling in the gaps. Handicapped writers could record on tape or dictate their initial accounts in order to determine their ability to observe and visualize.

If this first exercise gives evidence of poor observation on the part of many students, other exercises might follow on topics such as local landmarks, how to get to another part of the school, evidence of the coming of spring or fall, or impressions of a famous character from a television show. There is little hope that students can visualize scenes or descriptions written by others if they cannot reconstruct the details of their own environment. Some students may be so preoccupied with personal problems that they become blind to their own surroundings.

Students often learn to be more observant by writing about a wide variety of pictures of their own choice. Art can teach the observer about different aspects of a subject and different relationships within a structure as demonstrated by the collages in Chapter 4. Since good categorizing depends on good observation, this kind of training is far from being a frill. Combining good observation with thinking and writing activities is possible by assigning creative writing in conjunction with description. The following form of questioning has proved popular and makes a learning station possible.

Some students have problems with the mechanics of writing and they may benefit from taping their answers first and then getting aid in writing them.

Many visualizing activities are possible in other classrooms. In social studies, students may prepare maps, graphs, or drawings from a description. After being instructed to watch a full weather report on television, students can superimpose a weather map on a U.S. map according to written directions. In math, students can represent a math problem graphically. Packaged materials are also available with visualizing exercises, but the tasks must be related to the curriculum.

WRITING ABOUT A PICTURE

(Number the answers on your own paper. There is no need to copy the questions.)

1. Look at the picture very carefully. What was the first thing you thought of when you saw the picture?
2. List as many people, objects, and shapes as you see in the picture.
3. What is the mood of the picture? (happy, sad, funny, frightening, thoughtful, quiet, noisy, suspenseful)
4. If the picture is in color, what is the most important color?
5. What other colors do you see?
6. If the picture is black and white, is there more black, more white, or about an equal amount of each?
7. If there are people in the picture, list details about them under headings such as, *Boy, Old Man, Young Woman.*
8. If there are people in the picture, what expressions do they have on their faces? (happy, sad, frightened, thoughtful, ashamed, cruel, kind, angry, disappointed)
9. If there are animals in the picture, list details about them under a good heading. Do their faces show expression?
10. If the picture is abstract, do any of the shapes remind you of something? Can you sketch the most important shapes or lines in the picture?
11. Now read over everything you have written. Make up your own title for the picture.
12. You are ready to write about your own thoughts and feelings. Here are some suggestions.
    a. Write about what the picture means to you.
    b. Write about something it reminds you of.
    c. Write a story that occurs to you when you look at the picture.
    d. Write a poem about the picture or describe your feelings after looking at it.

In literature, there are many visualizing examples. Not all students can draw pictures well, but many can sketch floor plans or draw rough maps. In other cases, students can collect details about a character in a book, then write a brief description from memory. When a student has visualized details, this assignment is easy. A shadowy shape has gradually come into focus while reading. Details and sense impressions of all kinds are essential elements for the task. Students may receive aid initially by filling in given categories as they read: *Height and Weight; Color of Hair; Eyes; Complexion; Way of Speaking, Laughing, Moving; Type of Personality; Special Skills or Occupation;* and *Other.*

Imagination is necessary also for predicting behavior. As a good reader progresses in an account, he starts to predict what will happen next, and this prediction heightens his interest. If the development is largely psychological, the reader has to understand feelings and states of mind. Understanding the significance of certain details comes largely with experience. Thirteen- and fourteen-year-olds often are left quite cold by stories other than adventure or science fiction. Learning to predict through visualizing details can be encouraged, however. Reading or playing a recording of an exciting story and breaking off at the most exciting moment to ask for predictions is a good way to get an argument going. The only way to settle the argument is to *read* the ending.

□ *What reinforcement activities are essential in order to assure retention and use of this system for both reading and writing?*

Writing paragraphs

Once the categorizing exercises and the essay have been completed, application of the learned skills can begin. Regardless of the subject matter being studied, students can apply the process of collecting and organizing ideas and translating them into paragraphs. It should be stressed again that it is not necessary for the teacher to evaluate every word written. Weekly examples written under controlled conditions can be checked to determine each student's progress. Students working in groups may check one another's productions, thereby gaining additional practice in evaluation.

Turning paragraphs into categories

Reading practice should receive careful supervision at first. Paragraphs complete with topic sentences can be turned into categories. At first, the teacher must point out these paragraphs, gradually moving toward having students make their own decisions after they have shown their ability to do so. In many instances, there will not be complete agreement on which is the topic sentence since some writers occasionally say something in two different ways and others write badly. The right and wrong aspect is far less important than the thinking. A sentence which deals only with specific items is clearly not a topic sentence. An orderly way of recording work is very helpful, for example:

Title of book or magazine _____	Date of publication _____
Chapter or other heading _____	
Page (s) _____	
Paragraph no. ____	Label _____
	Items _____
	_____
	_____
	_____

Topic sentence is the _____.

It is especially important to allow time for free, enjoyable reading or browsing when highly structured reading exercises are being stressed. The long-term goal of developing good individual reading habits must always be kept in mind. Limiting the amount of structured reading practice and varying activities within a class period can prevent unpleasant impressions. Small doses given often work best. Contract arrangements with students can make individualizing reading assignments much easier. It is possible to offer a choice of two or three programs for a marking period. No student should skip the steps in thinking processes, but some can choose to do more and work faster. Even the brightest students need systematic, structured guidance to become good readers.

Reading and writing related to practical tasks

Teachers rightly feel that poor readers need relief from written material in some classes in order to be successful at something. Much can be said for this argument against reading and writing in practical courses, such as industrial arts. However, a certain amount of reading and writing related to practical tasks is highly meaningful. Students, then, *need* to read. If important vocabulary is discussed first, as described in Chapter 4, some reading of this type is possible for all students. If there are numerous poor readers in the class, the teacher can first read the instructions slowly while students follow in the text. He can point out how to refer back to the instructions while working, based on the organization on the page (e.g., numbering or lettering, dark type, spacing, or underlining).

In addition to reading instructions, practical courses offer many opportunities for grouping tools and materials, describing care of equipment, writing directions or explanations for others, making labels, and ordering processes. Instead of handing out safety instructions, teachers can first have each student or a group write a set, then discuss a plan. When the plan has been duplicated, students can proofread it for errors. Other opportunities for reading and writing come when demonstrations, back-to-school nights, fashion shows, art shows, and concerts take place. All discussions of orderly procedures help to reinforce orderly thinking which, in turn, helps reading.

The preceding comments also apply to math and science. More preparatory time usually should be devoted to basic vocabulary. Writing sentence problems and exchanging them, categorizing the elements of problems, and writing procedures can all reinforce the reading program. The classification system in science is the model of categorizing. Exercises in filling in categories with additional items, writing labels for groups of items, writing brief paragraphs on process, or outlining cause and effect sequences are all important contributions to the thinking that underlies reading.

Similar opportunities exist in the study of foreign languages. Grouping new vocabulary under suitable labels helps students associate words, especially if they have already mastered one of them. Instead of standard fill-in or matching tests, items can be placed under labels, some of which will be new and require careful thinking. Many of the newer texts make use of excellent procedures to improve students' thinking patterns.

Social studies combines all the elements discussed and, carefully planned, can reinforce all thinking skills. Not only are reading and writing essential but maps, charts, and graphs are also used which involve fundamental concepts of time, space, and numbers. Crucial to helping students think and, therefore, read better are an awareness of underlying concepts, the need for association with the students' lives, and the importance of introducing new material in such a way that patterns and groups of ideas are clear.

Other opportunities exist for the application of categorizing. One is making opinion polls about a subject under study, such as energy uses, pollution control, or how people feel about cities. After initial reading and research on the topic, groups brainstorm the subject; then, they pool their ideas, choose major categories, and write questions. When the data is brought in, it is valuable to tabulate it and make charts or graphs to represent the results. Students could be asked to predict some of the results and give the basis for these predictions. Results of a small, unrepresentative group (e.g., fathers only) could be tabulated separately and compared with the total. This process includes the following thinking activities: looking at a topic from all sides, selecting major areas for study, formulating factual rather than loaded questions, and organizing results and representing them graphically. The comparison of a small sample with a large one may encourage critical reading of political and advertising claims. Thinking, reading, writing, and translating a vague idea on a topic into a one-page chart are all included. A final activity can be the writing of a brief report.

□ *Can other aspects of language development*
  and usage be incorporated into this system as
  aids to better reading and writing?

Chapter 4 presents a discussion of how vocabulary study and outlining can be connected with categories. In the following pages, a few relationships signaled by function words will be touched upon to illustrate other ways a systematic approach can be used.

Function words, whose sole purpose is to signal particular relationships between ideas, are very abstract; by themselves they cannot be associated with mental images but must be associated with particular mental operations. These operations need to be understood as clearly as vocabulary words are understood to stand for concepts.

Conjunctions and sentence structure

In previous activities, students wrote topic sentences and simple sentences based on one specific item. The purpose of this exercise was to familiarize students with a basic system for organizing ideas. Most of their reading, however, will include complex and compound sentences. In order to understand the mental processes used in constructing such sentences, students first need to learn how to combine their own after watching a demonstration.

The demonstration can refer to three sample paragraphs on the topic *red* or can be based on textbook material. When completed, the students can try combining sentences in their own essays as a first exercise. It is essential to caution against combining the topic sentence with sentences based on specific items, since they have different functions in a paragraph.

Three types of conjunction, or joining, techniques can be shown by working with the *red* paragraphs.

RED

1. There are many examples of red seen in nature. Flowers are sometimes red. Even animals are occasionally red. Rubies are a kind of red stone.

2. Red comes in many shades from very light to very dark. Pink is often used for baby girls. Orange is easily seen and is sometimes used for uniforms or safety clothing. Burgundy is very dark.

3. Sometimes red is used as a symbol. When driving we have to stop at a red light or stop sign. A red flag shows danger. A red cross is a sign for medical help.

Paragraph 1. The topic sentence must not be combined with others and the fourth one does not lend itself to easy combination. The second and third sentences, however, share a predicate, "are sometimes (occasionally) red." A simple *and* can combine them: "Flowers *and* even animals are sometimes red." In this case, the word *and* functions like a plus sign.

Paragraph 2. The second and third sentences in this paragraph share the verb *used*, but the case is not like paragraph 1 because the third sentence has two parts joined by *and. While* is a possible conjunction in its sense, "at the same time; that is, in a similar manner" (Webster). *While* is an "in-between" word. The sentences would read: "Pink is often used for baby girls while orange is easily seen and is sometimes used for uniforms or safety clothing."

Paragraph 3. The last two sentences in this paragraph present a new problem. One of these statements can be looked upon as being negative, the other positive. For this reason *and* is inappropriate. If this conjunction is suggested, it should be tried and an attempt made to encourage criticism. A more appropriate word is *but,* already mentioned in Chapter 4. "A red flag shows danger, *but* a red cross is a sign for medical help."

It is beyond the scope of this book to go into detail on all conjunctions. Every one of them represents far more than a technical way of combining thoughts. Conjunctions represent fundamental, logical relationships. Students who do not understand how to use them will have problems understanding what they read. Misuse of *and* may indicate poor categorizing which results from not seeing that two items have little in common (e.g., adding apples and bananas). Misuse of *but* may indicate an inability to distinguish positive from negative statements within a given frame of reference.

Once more we find that it is relationships among ideas that cause so many comprehension problems. The temptation is to say, "The students are never going to understand this anyway." The trouble with that attitude is that it is a self-fulfilling prophecy. Function words are found on every page of secondary level reading and must be understood. As with basic categorizing, this involves using concrete ways of conveying abstract notions. Making large representations of all the conjunctions and having students physically carry them and suitably place them would be a good way of dramatizing the importance of the words. Some students may find it interesting to create figures to represent the relationships. One way of doing this is to cut cardboard into three or four basic shapes in different colors and to combine these. It may be assumed that thoughts move from left to right (see the basic shapes illustrated).

Various games might be useful for those students having severe problems with relationships. One game requires each student to write basic words with felt-tip pens on file cards. The words should be legible from the front of the room. A student reads a passage after having practiced beforehand. Each time a function word is read, all students should hold up that card. At first, the reader can pause for each function word. As the students practice and become accustomed to the exercise, no pause should be made. By isolating these words temporarily, teachers can help students become aware that they too are signals for a particular kind of mental action. After a while *because* should signify: "Look for the *cause* of what went before," if it comes in the middle of a sentence. If it comes at the beginning, it signals: "Look for the cause up to the comma, then the effect."

Jody liked Mr. Grub *because* he always gave her candy.
Because Mr. Grub always gave her candy, Jody liked him.

Basic Shapes

 = and    = as a result,
                                                because
                   One thought is built on the other.

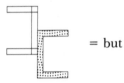 = but   The positive thought is stopped by
                                 the word, which at the same time
                                 reopens the thought negatively.
                                 Ideas joined are never exact opposites.

                                  = either . . . or

 = in spite of, although,
                      regardless, etc. The
                      thought continues through
                      the obstacle.

(Positive and negative elements should not be black and white, but red and green or some other color combination.)

Adverbs and prepositions

Other function words, when understood, enhance student abilities to visualize what is being read. Most of these are adverbs or prepositional phrases. In a court of law, it can make a great difference whether the witness says, "I saw him go *to* the house," or "I saw him go *into* the house." All students can read *in* and *into*, but what do they see when they read these little words? Brief descriptions can be written by students using certain words from a list. Other students can then illustrate these on the chalkboard, under the watchful eyes of the author and fellow students. Here is an example:

> There was a house *in* the field. *Around* it was a fence. *Near* the house was a stream. A small pier jutted *into* the stream. Some hills could be seen *far away behind* the house. A few small trees grew *here* and *there*.

A system similar to the one suggested for vocabulary words could be incorporated into the vocabulary notebook. Rather than using or stressing the names of parts of speech, the usefulness of these words for particular tasks can be shown in the label. Students can be encouraged to refer to these pages of their notebook when writing. Examples of headings are:

1. Words useful for joining ideas—conjunctions
2. Words which help the reader visualize—adverbs, prepositions

Creative writing activities can be combined with the study of different kinds of function words. Groups can write and act out skits while their classmates write down all the words that perform a certain function. These might be conveying a sense of time, place, manner, degree, number, or quality. The posttest for all the skits would be the correct categorizing of these words in a reading passage.

☐ *Can students derive other systems of organization from a thorough understanding of how categories are built and used in reading and writing?*

So far, simple categories have been translated into simple paragraphs having the topic sentence at the beginning. Obviously, reading is not made up entirely of this kind of paragraph. For various reasons, such as emphasis or a desire to vary the style, the topic sentence may come after the item sentences or in the middle. Some paragraphs are purely descriptive or transitional and require no topic sentence. Students will need practice in writing and reading these different kinds of paragraphs.

Other structures need special attention. While a grasp of both the categorizing process and the different ways in which categories can be related should give students the ability to recognize one kind of structural form in reading, other relationships and the words that signal them need careful teaching. What follows is not an exhaustive discussion but rather an introduction to a few relationships and ways of identifying and understanding them.

Once again, teachers may ask why it is necessary to discuss structures which students use in daily conversation. Experience has shown that use of function words (*because, if, or*) with familiar concepts does not always equip people to understand the same structures in an unfamiliar setting. At times, the structures are spread over several paragraphs or pages and are not necessarily clearly signaled. As he reads, the student must create a meaningful framework in his mind in order to place the ideas in proper relationship.

Cause and effect statements

A simple *because* sentence, such as "The bottle exploded *because* of excessive heat," may not be hard to understand, but cause and effect sequences that are more extensive often cause problems. In order to have a clear idea of which causes precipitated an effect, students have to be able to recognize both parts of the structure and test the validity of the assumptions. Is it likely that the stated or implied *cause* brought about the stated *effect*? Examples are "I got a D on the test because the teacher doesn't like me," or "The Depression was caused by the decadence of society at that time."

Cause and effect are not always clearly presented as such. In novels and short stories, the sequences may be more implied than stated. The leading question is "*Why* did (was, were)?" A textbook or novel may describe a series of events chronologically without stating what was cause and what was effect. Students may find it very helpful to group the events by choosing important ones and asking "Why did this happen?" This grouping will best be expressed differently from a simple category even though a label could be *Causes of X Event*. A better way to express the particular structure is to outline it in reverse order. Here are two examples:

1.	causes	heavy rains
		inadequate drainage
		+ shallow river banks
	effect	flood

2.	causes	Shane is forced to use a gun
		+ Shane becomes too involved
	effect	Shane leaves

Several examples of these sequences should be read and outlined, and key words which reveal these structures should be discussed. *Why* as the leading question and *because* as the simplest signal have already been mentioned. *As a result, events leading up to,* and *this resulted in* are frequently found.

Conditional statements

Students are very familiar with conditional statements at home and school: "If you don't clean your room, you won't go to the movies," "If you don't do your homework, you won't be able to pass the course." These statements always imply a threat. (They also anticipate a cause and effect situation. "Because you didn't clean your room, you can't go to the movies." "Because you didn't do your homework, you have flunked the course.") The big signal for this structure is the word *if.* The entire signal is *if . . . then,* but the second part is often just implied. The signal *if* should alert the reader to ask, "What will happen if this is done?" In logic and mathematics, conditional statements have to do with proving relationships. "*If* you add only even numbers, *then* the total will be an even number." The two parts of the statement, which may be an extended statement expressed in more than one sentence or paragraph, can be paraphrased under the headings

if	*then*
you don't clean your room	you won't go to the movies
you add all even numbers	the total will be an even number

Listing in this way may make more sense for some reading passages than traditional outlining. Again, this type of structure needs to be identified and studied.

Alternation statements

The word *or* is often used between commas with another word or phrase to indicate a paraphrase of a previous statement. "Translating symbols into sounds, *or* decoding, is the first step in reading." More typically, the word *or* signals a choice and always implies or is combined with the word *either*. This *either . . . or* construction is closely related to conditional (*if . . . then*) or cause and effect (*because*) statements and to positive and negative comparisons. It represents either a forced choice or alternative explanations or predictions.

"If you don't clean your room, you won't go to the movies." can be expressed as, "*Either* you clean your room, *or* you don't go to the movies." The two halves of this type of statement can either be both positive, both negative, or one positive and the other negative.

The *either . . . or* construction is often used when explaining events. A meeting in town is arranged. One party does not appear. The other one perhaps thinks, "*Either* her watch is slow *or* she got caught in traffic." (The *either* is often omitted.) The construction is also sometimes tied in with cause and effect statements. "The cake burned *either because* the oven was too hot *or because* it was left in too long." This type of sentence may appear very simple to a good reader, but it presents great problems to the reader who has not thoroughly grasped the mental operations required whenever the signals *either, or*, and *because* are seen. The simplest way out for a poor reader is omit these words mentally, even if they are spoken. What is left is, "The cake burned . . . the oven was too hot . . . it was left in too long." The reader gets the gist of things, but he does not grasp the relationships.

The *either . . . or* structure for predicting fits the student exercise of predicting what will happen next in a story. Students can be asked to make a sentence: "I think that Robin will *either* fly back to earth *or* he will make friends with the Munchers." To this can be added a *because* clause: "*because* nothing bad ever happens to the hero." The exercise would be very meaningful if columns made on the board were labeled EITHER, OR, and BECAUSE. There should be considerable interest in finding out which prediction is correct. Later, students can write other examples. These can be connected to the curriculum, e.g., "Washington wrote Congress that *either* money should be sent immediately *or* no one should expect his army to be able to fight."

A game can be devised to help fix the function of the signals *either* and *or* in students' minds. Since the words indicate a choice, the game must also represent a choice in the presence of the two signals. Two decks of small file cards should have the word OR printed conspicuously on the back of one deck and the word EITHER printed on the back of the other deck. Students can discuss and agree on the content of the statements to be written on the reverse side of the cards. It is important that some statements be positive and some negative in order to represent different *kinds* of choices: 1) between two positive situations, 2) between two negative situations, and 3) between one of each. Students should all get a turn before the tasks are begun. When a player has turned over one EITHER and one OR card, he should read the statements aloud and then rephrase them as, "I must *either* do . . . *or* . . . ," then declare his choice. Small groups can also play this game.

The game will be much more meaningful if students have written the cards. Each student can produce one card for each deck. If the class is divided into three groups, a group can be assigned choices 1, 2, or 3 to ensure variety. (This aspect of the game also reinforces earlier activities with positive and negative concepts.) When the cards are completed, each deck should be shuffled and the backs placed all in the same direction. A few suggestions for possible statements follow:

1. Cleaning up chores in the classroom, tidying books or files, completing learning stations, making an illustration for a short poem, writing a paragraph or poem about a picture, describing why you like a person, making something for the bulletin board, memorizing a verse and reciting it to the class, correctly writing words which are often misspelled, completing a map.

2. Getting out of classroom chores, being first in line for lunch, taking the next message to the office, being excused from homework for one day, teaching a spelling word to the class.

3. Standing on one foot for two minutes, not talking for two minutes, not smiling for two minutes, closing eyes for two minutes, looking surprised for one minute, singing a nursery rhyme or other song, choosing a partner for a five-minute conversation, walking the length of the room five times.

Negative statements

The discussion of *either* . . . *or* statements leads logically to negative structures such as *neither* . . . *nor* sentences or situations. In

Chapter 4, the word *no* was chosen to head the list of negative concepts, directly below the minus sign. Students understand fully a simple negative answer to a question using the word *no,* but many do not understand that the same word within a sentence completely reverses an otherwise positive statement. For example, "There will be *no* school today," means the exact opposite of "There will be school today." Some students simply overlook the word, perhaps because they are uncertain of its function. The problem in reading is then twofold: 1) the word or similar words must be noticed and 2) once noticed, the word's function must be clear to the reader.

The negative word list from the Chapter 4 exercise on positive and negative words can be reviewed for the ones which function to reverse meaning. *Not* and *never* function the same way as *no* and *neither . . . nor,* although *never* introduces a time element lacking in the other words and often implies, "never, unless . . . ." Any of these words can be inserted or deleted in a statement without changing anything else. Other negative words function only in connection with implied positive concepts (or the other way around). Inserting or deleting them requires changing other aspects of the sentence. Such words are *none, nobody,* and *nothing* which imply the words *some, somebody,* and *something* as possibilities in the same situation. "*Nobody* went to the meeting" implies that *somebody* might have gone. "There was *nothing* to eat" implies a possibility that there might have been *something* to eat.

Besides words that reverse the meaning of sentences, there are certain prefixes that reverse the meaning of words. *Un-, non-,* and *dis-* are examples. *Un*pleasant means the opposite of pleasant. If a vocabulary notebook is used in the way suggested earlier, these negative prefixes should be grouped together.

Helping students become aware of the function of negative words and prefixes should start with examples from daily life. Making either positive or negative statements and having students alter them by inserting or deleting negative words is useful but should be accompanied by actual physical movements. A series of directions including both kinds of statements can be used as a demonstration. Learning the negative signals can be combined with the EITHER-OR game, since negative choices can be indicated by using negative signals.

When combined with other function words in a sentence, negative words create highly complex structures. An example is "He was *not* in love with her, *but* he enjoyed her company and spent much of his time with her." The possible inference of this sentence is,

"Some people might think he is in love with her because he spends so much time with her but, in fact, he just enjoys her company." Another example is, "He was *never* lazy, but family worries made him absentminded and caused him to neglect his job." Again, there is an implication of possible misunderstanding.

The importance of grasping the function of negative words is demonstrated by the number of errors made on test questions such as "Which group of words does not represent a correct sequence?" More importantly, readers are handicapped on almost every page if they are unaware of the crucial role of the negative signals, especially significant in practical directions. Overlooking the *not* in the direction, "Do not press the button unless the valve is open," could be disastrous.

Double negatives can be dealt with in conjunction with negative statements. Since most students understand that two minuses make a plus, this analogy can be used. Once all the negative words and prefixes have been identified, sentences can be analyzed according to the number of negative or minus statements. When two minus signs can be indicated, the statement must *either* be considered positive *or* changed to eliminate one minus.

Examples:

1. "I ain't going to do it no how!"
   $(-)$ $(-)$

   Either this means, "I will do it."

   Or the statement must be changed to "I won't do it."
        $(-)$

2. "Not enough uniforms had not yet arrived to outfit the Continental Army."
   $(-)$ $(-)$

   Either this means, "Enough uniforms had arrived to outfit the Continental Army."

   Or the statement must be changed to "Not enough uniforms had arrived to outfit the Continental Army."
         $(-)$

   Or "The uniforms had not yet arrived to outfit the Continental Army."

Review

The function words in these pages need to be emphasized, isolated, and examined. In a limited way, they can be compared to the operator symbols in math which tell the reader whether to add, subtract, multiply, or divide given numbers. Language is less precise than math, and one symbol, or signal, can stand for a variety of activities in different situations. The specific mental activity required when a signal is seen on the page should be understood. Once this has been done, however, it is equally important to ensure that the words take their place among all the others in contributing to meaning. Writers do not use function words for their own sake, but only to establish relationships among ideas they wish to communicate.

As a review of function words, reading assignments should include many different kinds of structures and signal words related to the curriculum. Before requiring individual analysis of reading passages, one example should be worked through with a class or group. This can be done so that poor readers may take part in the discussion when the teacher reads a sentence aloud and asks for identification of any signal words. After identification, students can discuss further the specific mental activity required by the signal words.

For individual reading assignments, questions should be asked along these lines:

1. Find a word that signals a negative statement joined to a positive statement in a sentence. Write in your own words.
   a. *positive statement*   b. *negative statement*   signal word _____

2. Find a word that signals a cause and effect relationship. Summarize the statement.
   a. *causes*   b. *effect*   signal word _____

3. Find a negative word that reverses the meaning of a sentence. Rewrite the statement in a positive way.
   signal word _____

4. Find a word that signals alternatives. What are the choices? Write them in your own words.
   a. *one choice*   b. *another choice*   signal word _____

5. Find a word that signals a condition to be met. Write in your own words.
   a. *result*   b. *condition*   signal word _____

It may be necessary to tape passages for poor readers or have passages read aloud to small groups. Again, the object of the assignment is not so much individual mastery of every word as it is the ability to understand the relationships among ideas expressed. Poor readers should also be allowed to ask the meaning of vocabulary words.

Continuing ways to improve reading

Previewing

Reading well does not consist of simply putting together a number of separate skills. Ultimately, all skills are subordinate to the highly complex integration of the reader's personal experience and way of thinking, the writer's ability to communicate his ideas, and hundreds of interlocking mental activities all combining to produce one perception of the text. All these elements cannot be brought together into a workable review sheet. It is possible, though, to group certain elements common to most types of reading and to make students aware of important work to be done before and during reading. When students have engaged in a number of mental processes described in this chapter, they might find additional help from the use of a student reading review sheet similar to the sample shown.

Some items on the sheet, such as "number and quality of illustrations," require students to *evaluate* material. This procedure needs to be introduced in class first in order to point out criteria for judging the items. The ability to evaluate reading material becomes very important in the upper grades.

STUDENT READING REVIEW SHEET

Previewing a Book, Periodical, Encyclopedia Article, Magazine
1. author's purpose _____
2. author's intended audience _____
3. author's style _____
4. date of publication _____
5. author's qualifications _____
6. preview of introduction _____
7. preview of conclusion _____
8. organizational structure _____ (chapters, units, sections)
9. index _____
10. table of contents _____
11. useful appendices, glossary _____
12. number and quality of illustrations, charts, etc. _____

Previewing Important Signals on a Particular Page
1. spacing _____
2. differences in print size or shape _____
3. use of color _____
4. capitalizing and punctuation _____
5. use of numbers and letters to order ideas _____
6. illustrations, charts, etc. _____
7. main topics covered _____

Previewing a Particular Paragraph

1. purpose of paragraph _____
2. presence or absence of topic sentence and its position _____
3. logical order of items _____
4. logical structure of the paragraph _____
5. key words that reveal this structure _____
6. inferences or unstated conclusions _____
7. key words conveying these _____
8. transition phrase or sentence relating this paragraph to previous or following paragraphs _____

Peer teaching

Some schools have been successful at organizing peer teaching for the benefit of those needing immediate help and for those needing to reinforce skills. Any fledgling reader who has mastered a particular skill should be eligible to assist others who are less skilled. In some schools, students can also choose peer teaching for credit instead of another elective. Using student power in this way can greatly reduce behavior problems by assuring necessary individual attention. As always, careful training is essential, and clear goals are necessary. No teacher should be forced to accept peer teachers nor should the activity be looked upon as a salvation for scheduling problems. Peer teaching can contribute greatly to reading progress; in addition, because *any* student who has mastered a skill has a chance to serve, there is no snobbish status assigned to those participating.

Parent help

It is often true that it is hard to make contact with the parents of students who need help most. Sometimes this is due to short-sighted scheduling of opportunities for contacts. Some parents cannot afford to miss work, and some work at night. Sending notes home about help needed is time-consuming for teachers, but no more so than sending notes about discipline problems which have to be discussed. These problems may be reduced by communication between parents and teachers before trouble starts.

Often parents have no idea that their child's reading will be improved if there is more *conversation* at home. Trips around town and into the country or visits with relatives offer golden opportunities for talking about road signs, rivers and streams, railroads, and interstate highways. Where do things come from? Where do they go? Using maps for trips is very helpful. Are we going north, south, east, or west? How would we know if there were no maps? Discussing news and weather reports, planning purchases, or arranging a party can provide other opportunities for conversation.

Many homes have tape recorders. Fellow students can prepare weekly instructional tapes of vocabulary words or other needed skills. Review sheets for specific tasks or tests can be sent home by agreement. During the summer, students and their parents can sign contracts for specific reading tasks such as reading one paragraph of the sports page every day, watching the news or one of the educational television programs, or preparing for a course by learning the basic vocabulary ahead of time.

Conclusion

The goal of all the activities described in this book is to produce readers who make maximum use of their natural endowments. Some will learn how to read newspapers and directions; others will be able to enjoy James Baldwin, Henry James, or Bertrand Russell. Not all students will need extensive practice in every skill since they may already have mastered them. Mastery should be proved, however, not taken for granted. Every student will need to understand these aspects of reading:

1. The importance of careful observation with all the senses.
2. The fact that all items can be categorized in many different combinations.
3. The way ideas are grouped and then ordered in hierarchies, and the function of certain words in revealing relationships between ideas or groups of ideas.
4. The function of other words in conveying the writer's vision to the mind of the reader.
5. The ways in which the printed page provides special signals to activate particular mental activities.

The key word in reading is *action*. Every symbol on the page demands action, including the empty spaces which function like rests in music: to set off and emphasize certain sounds and symbols.

Research in reading methods so far has "proved" only that there are many roads to Mecca and that the personality of the teacher and the systematic use of *a* method are factors which influence success. The method advocated throughout this book is based on what is known about how people learn and remember, as well as upon the special psychological needs of pre- and early adolescents. The major thesis is that concepts must be assimilated into the existing concept system of a person in order to be useful. Obviously, any one suggestion for linking new ideas to old will not work with every student. A variety of approaches may be necessary. Failure with one attempt should not lead to blind assumptions of the limitations of students and one success does not imply intellectual brilliance. There is great danger in permanently labeling students. Either the low expectation becomes a self-fulfilling prophecy or the high expectation means that students are not given necessary mental tools or opportunities to develop emotionally while leaping ahead intellectually.

Once separate skills have been learned, only a great deal of practice in integrating them in actual reading experiences can bring about automatic reaction to specific clues. These reading experiences need to be of two kinds: 1) those directed to a specific goal within a subject context; and 2) those entirely of a person's own choosing. The first will help introduce the reader to different ways of approaching understanding of particular subject matter; the second will allow the reader to enjoy the activity and, therefore, to *want* to read. If schools are serious about improving reading, they should prove it by devoting class time to both kinds of reading. Both faculty and administration need to understand the reading process and support a program designed to improving reading.

Different approaches to specific reading tasks are covered in many books on reading. Herber and other authors write about reading tasks in relation to particular subjects. Broadly, the main categories are: finding facts (items), main ideas (labels), inferences and unstated conclusions, and understanding vocabulary. The area which is beginning to get more attention involves the thinking process and the signals which activate particular processes. That is the area especially covered in this book.

All new information and skills must be related to concepts already absorbed. Instruction tends to be a waste of time when this is not done. Why is it that students are said to forget 80 percent of what is taught during twelve years of schooling? Any activity not involving sitting at a desk with pen, paper, and book at hand is considered a waste of time by many schools. Time spent discovering the strengths of students is not wasted. Time spent filling out worksheets, with multiple-choice or haphazard fill-in questions about little understood facts presented in isolation, may well be wasted. A neat piece of paper may indicate only a neat piece of paper.

Piaget and others have demonstrated the importance of play in learning: "Play is child's work." *Play* means finding out, trying out, investigating, manipulating, and making decisions. It is slowly being acknowledged that even adults need to play. Early adolescents, because of their preoccupation with social relationships, certainly need opportunities to learn by playing. This book has attempted to show some playful ways of encouraging reading comprehension. Surely, reading and those who teach it should have neither a grim and unpleasant nor a falsely ingratiating image. Reading will not improve where respect for the student as a human being is absent. Respect requires finding the student's "starting place."

Play is a deadly serious occupation. In some countries adult spectators kill each other over a game. Persons who have watched children absorbed in games will ignore the evidence if they say, "It's just a game." Playful ways of learning are advocated seriously in this book. Students making up their own games or playing games according to agreed criteria are not wasting time if the goals have been carefully thought through.

The ideas expressed here are intended as an additional resource for teachers and others who want to understand why students have reading problems and who have an interest in helping all students learn to read better. The theoretical foundation for suggested techniques is that language must be associated with reality in particular patterns, such as categories, before these patterns can be recognized in reading. The practical application is a step-by-step advance from concrete experiences to abstractions leading to manipulation of written language. Growth in thinking abilities, together with a wider perspective gained through carefully guided activities, should lead to improved reading comprehension.

Student Glossary*

Abstract   Not found in nature or the environment; not real; something which people have thought up, often having to do with patterns or groups. The opposite is *concrete*, or real.

Abstract words   Term used to describe words for which you cannot have any picture in your mind. These words are often used to describe relationships among ideas or groups of ideas. Examples are *but, near, before,* and *because.* These are also function words.

Advertising   Words, pictures, television scenes, songs, and symbols used to influence a person to buy something or to join an organization.

Alphabetical order   Arranging words in the order of the alphabet. *Ace* will come before *at* or *bad.*

Alternation statements   Statements in two parts, the first part introduced by *either* (sometimes omitted), the second by *or.* These two statements always represent a *choice* of explanations or actions, and this choice can be between two positive, two negative, or one positive and one negative alternatives.

Analysis   The way we try to see the different parts of something and how they are related to each other and to the whole. We can just enjoy riding a bike, or we can *analyze* how all the parts of the bike work. If we have to repair the bike, the analysis is important. We also have to analyze language and ideas.

Appropriate   Suitable, fitting. Wearing your best clothes to a wedding is appropriate. Using your best, most formal language is appropriate for formal occasions, while using slang with your friends is also appropriate. Selecting appropriate items for a category or a label for a group of items is important.

Arbitrary order   A way of arranging things in an order which has nothing to do with logical grouping. Alphabetical and numerical order are often arbitrary. If you line up people alphabetically for a performance or parade, you will have tall and short people mixed together. Lining up by height would be *logical.*

*These words are defined only in the way they are used in this publication.

Aspect   A way of looking at something, either a real view of it from a particular place or a way of thinking about it. Aspects of a tree include the way it looks from all sides, near and at a distance, how it looks at different times of year, what kind of root system it has, how old it is, how large it is, how it is related to similar trees, and what it can be used for.

Association of ideas   The way ideas are linked or connected with other ideas in your mind. Somebody says TV and you think of potato chips or cookies. Association of ideas helps us to learn new things by connecting them to things we already know. It also helps us to collect ideas for writing.

Brainstorming   A way of getting as many ideas as possible about a particular object or problem. A group of people offer ideas in any order they come to mind, using association of ideas, different meanings of words, recall of sense impressions, emotions, scenes from television or books, personal experiences, and symbols connected with the subject. Each person in a group brings a different experience, and the full group gains more ideas than one person could offer.

Category   A group of items with a common characteristic, or something in common. A category is made up of both the group of items and the label used to describe what they have in common.

Cause   A reason why something happened.

Cause and effect relationship   Two or more events connected by the fact that some event was the reason for another event. The word *because* and the phrase *as a result of* are frequent signals of this kind of relationship: "I am late *because* my alarm clock didn't go off."

Chronological order   Arranging events by the order in which they happen *in time.*

Common characteristic   Something a group of items has in common. Things do not have to look alike to have a common characteristic. A palace, a tent, and a cave all provide shelter for people, so shelter is their common characteristic.

Communicate   To transfer ideas to other people, usually by means of language, but also by facial expression, gesture, art form, or symbolic signal.

Compare   To look for ways in which an item is like or unlike other items. *Comparison* always means looking for both similarities and differences and involves more than one item. Comparing is a form of analysis, of careful observation and thinking about categories.

Concentration   Directing or centering your attention completely on one object, idea, or process.

Concrete   Something *real* which can be measured or weighed. A concrete object is always *specific*, never general.

Conditional statement   One or more sentences with an *if . . . then* idea (then is often omitted). A statement which tells under what conditions something will be true or will happen is a conditional statement:"*If* you eat contaminated or spoiled food, *then* you will become ill."

Connote   Suggesting a meaning beyond the literal, everyday meaning of a word or phrase. Examples are the use of "little woman" instead of wife or addressing a grown man who is not related to you as "son." In both cases, the expressions have the *connotation* that the speaker feels superior to the other person.

Consecutive   Following one another without gaps. "For seven consecutive days" means for seven days in a row.

Contrast   To stand out against something else, to be different, or to see the differences between objects or ideas. Light and shade, laughter and tears, poor and rich, are examples of contrast.

Degree   A member of a series arranged in steps, such as degrees of temperature or degrees of close or distant relationship between people.

Difference   The way in which something is not like something else. When you have to decide how to put things in categories, you look for differences and similarities.

Effect   Result of an event. An effect is *caused* by something else. "The *effect* of all his hard work was his winning the prize."

Efficient   Bringing about results without waste of time, energy, or material. An example is "Thinking in categories is an *efficient* way to learn."

Emotion   A strong feeling. Although closely related, an emotion is different from a sense impression because the latter is a physical reaction. For example, a fire can make you very hot or burn you, but you can also have the *emotions* of fear and excitement because of the fire. An emotion can be pleasant (joy) or unpleasant (sorrow).

Environment   Everything surrounding an individual. This includes the climate, type of vegetation, geographical features, family, housing, educational and job opportunities, and the culture. People know their environment first through their senses. It is a main force forming the character of an individual.

Experience   The ways in which each person's environment has affected him. New events, people, or ideas are learned by relating them to past experiences. Thinking about past experiences or events as they happen, and looking for ways to put them into categories, help people to understand new experiences. Past experiences can help people to predict what will happen.

Fact   Something that is done or exists about which you can ask the questions, who? what? when? where? how? how many? how much? Facts can be past events or statements about the environment. Not all statements are statements of fact; for example, "Everybody should learn how to grow food" is not a fact but an opinion. Other statements may be untrue and, therefore, not about facts. "Everybody loves to watch football on television," is an example.

Family tree   A diagram showing the way in which members of a family group are related. The diagram is called a tree because it starts with the first known couple and spreads out below, each line becoming longer (horizontally) than the last. Members of one generation (people about the same age) are shown on the same line. A family tree is an example of a *hierarchy*.

Flexible   Able to bend, change, or be influenced. When you categorize objects, people, or ideas, it is important to be flexible in order to see the many different ways in which something can be included in categories.

Form   The shape of something. It is used in this book with the word *function* to show that the shape, or form, of an object is directly related to the way it is used. *Form* and *function* are not opposites; each one is dependent on the other. The form of a pencil is decided by the way a human hand has to hold it as well as the need for a writing point.

Function   The action for which a person or thing is especially fitted, made, or trained. The function of a pair of scissors is to cut.

Function words   Those words that are used only to show relationships between ideas and that have little or no meaning by themselves. Examples are *and, but, to, on, if,* and *or.*

General   Something that can be said about a group of objects, people, ideas, or events. A statement about one or more common characteristics may be a general statement. The opposite of *general* is *specific.* In a category the general statement is the *label.*

Group   A collection of people, objects, ideas, or events which is seen as a unit, having a common characteristic. *Group* is another word for *category*. Grouping is the same as categorizing, though the label may not be expressed clearly.

Habit   A usual manner of behavior. If we often do something a certain way, it becomes a habit so that we no longer think about it. A large part of our daily behavior is a matter of habit. Habits can be either good or bad.

Heading   A title, not necessarily a main title of a book or chapter. A heading is like a label of a category since it tells the reader what the following sentences will have in common, but it may cover several categories.

Hierarchy   An arrangement of people or ideas into a series. A hierarchy often has to do with *authority*, the person at the top having the most to say about decisions. Family groups form hierarchies based on age groups. Ideas are arranged in hierarchies by order of importance—the most general at the top and the most specific at the bottom. In textbooks, there is a hierarchy consisting of the title, chapter headings, section headings, paragraphs, sentences, and words. All of these are parts of a whole, related in different ways.

Imply   To say something indirectly. Association is often used to make an *implication*. For example, "Bill is an excellent student and a great athlete, and Fred is his best friend," *implies* that Fred is also a good student and athlete or, at least, somebody special. Another form of implication is indicating a necessary result. The statement, "The Grants are coming with their fourteen-year-old son. Teenagers are usually hard to entertain." implies that the Grant boy will be a difficult guest.

Indent   "Denting in" a sentence from the margin. This is the usual signal for the beginning of a paragraph and should indicate to the reader, "Watch out! Here comes a new group of ideas."

Infer   Arriving at a conclusion by reasoning from the evidence, without having a statement of that conclusion. You may infer from actions. For example, if you see somebody carefully locking up valuables, you can infer that they suspect somebody may be dishonest. In reading, inference is often used as a general term for "reading between the lines," but the word expresses a direct connection with reasoning, rather than a reaction to particular words as in *connotation*. If you read, "Mr. Bloom always saw the gloomy side of everything," then you will infer that he was not a cheerful companion, probably not invited out much.

Inflexible   Rigid, not capable of changing or bending. (The prefix *in—* means *not* in this word.) In categorizing, an inflexible person is able to categorize something in only one way and is unable to see other aspects. An example is seeing a ruler only as an object for measuring flat surfaces, not as an object to assist in drawing straight lines, hitting someone, or propping something.

Information   Knowledge communicated to someone. Information has to do with actual facts and events, not with possibilities or imagined events. It is necessary for making accurate predictions. Reading and writing are important ways of communicating information.

Item   A separate particular in a series or group. Members of a category are items and are distinct from the category label. A useful general term for a large number of different things that can be categorized, items may be objects, people, processes, elements, or ideas. An item is always specific, never general. To itemize means to list the members of a group.

Label   A term that identifies an object or a group of objects. It is used to identify the common characteristic of a category, as distinct from the specific items in that category. Labels are very important for understanding relationships and for remembering.

Language   A systematic means of communicating ideas or feelings by the use of generally accepted sounds and symbols. The word now includes communication by gesture and between animals, but in this book it is used only for spoken and written human communication. Language plays an important role in human thought, allowing people to list items, label categories, express ideas in sentences and paragraphs, show many different kinds of relationships, and predict the future.

Lettering   Used in this book to describe the custom of placing letters in alphabetical order in front of items in a series of written ideas. The letters may be either captial for sections or small for details. All items in a series shown by *A, B, C,* or *a, b, c* lettering belong to the same category. This category is usually related to others which are numbered. For example, a Roman numeral *I* may be followed by *A, B,* etc. Or *A* may be followed by Arabic numerals *1, 2,* etc.

Logical order   Items presented in an order which makes sense for those items and any hierarchy of ideas which includes the items. This is in contrast to *arbitrary order,* such as alphabetical or numerical. Order is important in reading and writing because it reveals the relationship between items or between whole categories. For example, alphabetical order of presidents of the United States might include a list like Eisenhower, Jefferson, Nixon, and Washington.

Chronological order (order in time) would give you Washington, Jefferson, Eisenhower, and Nixon. Some types of logical order are based on chronology (time), geography (space), size, age, or condition.

Main idea   The essential or central point of a group of ideas. The main idea is separate from the facts presented. It is often like the label of a category, expressing a relationship or common characteristic. Sometimes it is stated in a topic sentence, an introduction, or a conclusion. Sometimes the reader or listener has to *infer* the main idea. It is always a *general* rather than a specific idea.

Material   What an object is made of as distinct from its form. Material can be the reason for categorizing objects, such as *Plastic Objects* or *Wooden Objects*.

Memory   The power or process of recalling or reproducing what has been learned or experienced. Vivid events are retained or remembered without any effort, but a person trying to learn has to make his own decision to remember. Items need to be properly grouped and labeled to be remembered. These categories then need to be related to categories already in a person's mind. Each person has a unique memory, just as he has had a unique experience.

Miscellaneous   Belonging to a number of groups, not all having one clear, common characteristic. *Miscellaneous Objects* means a group of objects so different that nothing can be said about them except that they are objects. It is a useful way of grouping items after all other attempts have failed.

Negative   A denial, prohibition, or refusal. A *negative statement* says "no" in some way. In math, a minus sign is used. *Negative* is the opposite of *positive*. Certain words can reverse a positive statement and make it negative. For example, "I will go" becomes "I will *not* go!" Some prefixes work the same way; "I like" becomes "I *dis*like." Descriptive words can have a negative, or bad, meaning, like *sloppy, brutal,* or *selfish*.

Numbering   Assigning numbers to items in a category or a series of categories. All items numbered consecutively belong to the same category or series. Numbered series are often related to lettered series (see "lettering").

Numerical order   An order made by numbering items consecutively. Examples are the pages of a book, chapter numbers, and "taking a number card" in a store and being waited on in turn. Numerical order may have a logical basis or it may be *arbitrary*, without logical reason.

Observe   To see, sense, notice, or realize something. This can be done only with the senses and must be done well if we want to categorize well. It is possible that we observe mostly those things we have learned to think about. A gardener will observe growing things in a garden very differently from someone unfamiliar with plant life. Good *observation* is important for predicting what may happen.

Opinion   A view or judgment based on personal experience and not necessarily proved by the facts of a situation. An opinion may be based on fact, but the word is usually used when there is no proof that a personal statement is the truth. A fact answers questions such as "What?" "Where?" "When?"An opinion answers questions such as "What do you think?" "Where do you think it is?" "When do you think it will happen?"

Organize   To cause or develop a structure, grouping items according to a system. To arrange elements into a whole of interdependent parts is to organize. When we write, we need to gather ideas, organize them into categories, order items within categories in a certain way, and order whole categories within a larger unit.

Outline   To indicate the shape, outer limits, features, or principal parts of something. In written material, an outline shows the main sections and subheadings, usually by numbering and lettering, and with different sizes of print. In an outline, an item close to the margin will be superordinate (above in importance) to an item farther away from the margin.

Paragraph   A group of sentences about a particular topic written consecutively and continuously and signaled by indenting (or leaving a space between paragraphs or groups of related sentences). The word *graph* comes from the Greek word meaning "to write," and the prefix *para-* means "beside" or "alongside of." Paragraphs are the basic way of indicating groups of ideas and usually have more than one sentence.

Paragraph form   A form indicated by indenting and then writing sentences continuously. *Paragraph form* is used to indicate the *function* of grouping ideas. A writer has to signal the organization of his ideas, and the reader has to observe this structure.

Patterns   Groupings, either natural, accidental, or designed. A pattern can be described by naming its common characteristic such as "She always behaves well," "They always fly in V-formation," "A series of squares placed diagonally and connected by circles," or "Alternating blue and white stripes." People need to look for patterns in order to understand and predict.

Positive   Good or affirmative, the opposite of *negative*. In math, positive numbers are represented by a plus sign or absence of a minus sign. In language, the key word is *yes*. Descriptive words such as *beautiful, kind,* and *intelligent* can also be positive.

Predict   To foretell on the basis of observation, experience, or scientific reasoning. The word is made up of the prefix *pre-*, "before," and part of the word *diction*, "to speak," meaning "to speak before" something happens. Good categorizing is essential to good prediction. Predicting on the basis of insufficient observation ("Nobody steals in our school.") or observation distorted by prejudice ("Teenagers are all noisy, untidy, and irresponsible.") will turn out badly in most instances.

Prejudice   An opinion (not a fact) arrived at without sufficient observation. The word comes from the prefix *pre-*, "before," and the word *judge*, and it means to judge before there is sufficient evidence. Everybody has prejudices about groups of things, such as certain kinds of food, music, or people. Prejudices distort our way of seeing things because we *predict* with insufficient information.

Problem solving   A systematic way of dealing with problems or difficult questions of all kinds. Problem solving can be divided into the following steps: 1) careful observation of the circumstances or elements involved; 2) analysis of what we observe, including grouping items in various ways; 3) thinking of all possible ways of solving the problem; 4) deciding on a way to solve the problem; and 5) working out the most efficient way to do it. Good observation and categorizing are essential to problem solving.

Process   The *way* in which something is done; a series of actions or operations leading to a particular result. Understanding *how* you learn, *how* you read or write, can help you to use those skills intelligently. The process of categorizing consists of these steps: 1) observing carefully, 2) finding common characteristics, and 3) naming the common characteristics. This categorizing process can be used to categorize anything.

Product   Something produced or made. The product of the process of communicating a group of ideas may be a paragraph or a group of paragraphs.

Propaganda   The spreading of ideas, information, or rumor for the purpose of helping or hurting a person, a cause, or an institution. Propaganda can take many forms such as advertising, starting rumors, or slanting news reports. It means telling only those parts of the truth that suit your purpose.

Reasons   Explanations that make some fact understandable; a logical defense of a suggestion or proposal. Statements that answer the question "why?" are reasons. Examples are "I had a good reason for being absent; I was sick." "When I heard the reason why he was so angry, I felt sorry for him."

Reasonable   Fair, having sound judgment, agreeable to reason. A reasonable way of reacting is one which is controlled by *thinking* more than by feeling. A reasonable suggestion is one based on a careful look at a situation.

Relate   To find or show a logical connection between one item and another, to see a relationship between different things, to be able to form categories by seeing common characteristics.

Research   Careful investigation or experimentation aimed at the discovery of facts, testing of theories, or seeing how facts and theories are applied. Usually, research involves reading about something after looking up headings in encyclopedias or library card catalogs. Research is necessary in order to make sure you have correct facts and have seen all sides of a question.

Senses   The means by which we know about our environment through seeing, hearing, touching, tasting, and smelling. We can learn to make better use of our senses and, therefore, to observe better. This can lead to improved categorizing.

Sense impressions   Images created as a result of the use of the senses and processing what is sensed, leading to a link with past experiences so that recognition will occur. Sense impressions often affect emotions. When writing, we use these impressions as a means of collecting ideas about a topic.

Sentence   A group of words expressing one or more related thoughts. A sentence normally contains somebody or something (subject) doing or being something (predicate). It is usually signaled by a capital letter and concluded with a period, question mark, or exclamation point. A sentence is the smallest unit expressing a complete thought. Sentences are usually grouped into paragraphs.

Sequence   A continuous or connected series. Sequence is one way of ordering events. Directions often are written in a sequence and numbered. Sequence can also refer to chronology or to how events have happened in time.

Similar   Alike, closely resembling. A word describing something which can be related to other things by common characteristics. The opposite of *similar* is *different*. When comparing things for the purpose of placing them in categories, we need to look for *similarities* and *differences*.

Sort   To put into a certain place or rank according to certain characteristics. *Sorting* is another way to say *grouping* and is part of the process of categorizing.

Specific   Something within a named category; something particular, often a detail. The opposite of *specific* is *general.*

Specific items   Objects, people, events, ideas, elements, processes, or features grouped by a common characteristic. Specific items can be things from the real world.

Structure   The parts or elements of a whole determined by the general character of the whole. *Structure* is different from *form* in that it is not necessarily visible. A car has a form which you can see; it also has a structure, much of which you cannot see. For example, there may be heavy steel reinforcements, not visible, but constructed to protect you in an accident. In reading, the structure is usually made up of categories related to each other in a particular way, such as a hierarchy.

Style   The way something is expressed in fashion, dance, painting, music, buildings, or language. The style used to express thoughts in language should be suitable to the purpose of the writer or speaker and should show the reader or listener something about that purpose. A humorous style is not suitable for a speech at a funeral.

Subcategories   Categories formed by using an item from a category as the label for a new, subordinate category. For example, under the label *Springtime,* you might list sunshine, rain, birds nesting, and flowers. A subcategory can be formed by turning *Flowers* into a label and listing daffodils, crocuses, and snowdrops.

Subordinate   Placed in a lower class, having less authority or rank than some other person or thing. In a category, the specific items are subordinate to the general label. The word *superordinate* is the opposite of *subordinate.*

Superordinate   Superior in rank, class, or status. In a category, the general label is superordinate to the specific items. The opposite of *superordinate* is *subordinate.*

Symbol   Something that stands for or suggests something else because of a relationship, association, convention, or accidental similarity. A national flag is a patriotic symbol. Printed letters and words are symbols for sounds. Numbers are also symbols. Diamonds are symbols for romance or wealth. When collecting ideas for writing, it is useful to think about symbols associated with the topic.

System   A related group of items, interacting in a regular way, forming a unified whole. A river *system* consists of the main river and all the streams and tributaries which flow into it. A *systematic* way of writing means making decisions about how to collect, organize, and use ideas to build paragraphs and larger units. Having a system is the opposite of doing things "any old way."

Texture   The way something feels or looks, such as hard, soft, smooth, or rough; one possible way of categorizing objects.

Title   A descriptive or general heading for a book, chapter, or other complete unit of writing. A title unifies a number of categories or an entire hierarchy of categories, while a label is the heading for only one category.

Topic   The subject of a speech, a conversation, or a piece of writing such as a theme. A topic is usually expressed in a title.

Vary   To make partial changes, as in the way you express a topic sentence, sometimes starting with the subject, sometimes starting with other parts of the sentence. *Variety* in writing stimulates interest rather than boredom in readers.

Bibliography*

COGNITIVE DEVELOPMENT

Bruner, J. S.   *The Process of Education.* Cambridge: Harvard University Press, 1960. A paper containing important passages on structure in learning and the need for understanding the foundations of any subject.

Dewey, J.   *Experience and Education.* New York: Macmillan, 1951. Dewey did not advocate haphazard experience for its own sake but rather a developmental "conscious articulation of facts and ideas." Highly readable.

Elkind, D.   *A Sympathetic Understanding of the Child Six to Sixteen.* Boston: Allyn and Bacon, 1971. A brief, general account of development by a leading American interpreter of Piaget. Includes useful "profiles" of each age.

Inhelder, B., and **J. Piaget.**   *The Growth of Logical Thinking from Childhood to Adolescence.* New York: Basic Books, 1958. Chapter 18 is especially helpful in showing the relationship between affective and intellectual development of adolescents.

Luria, A. R.   *The Working Brain: An Introduction to Neuropsychology.* New York: Basic Books, 1973. An excellent paperback containing the most important findings to date.

Piers, M. W. (Ed.).   *Play and Development.* New York: W. W. Norton, 1972. Papers from a symposium which included Piaget and Erikson. The epilogue raises important questions for education.

Wadsworth, B. J.   *Piaget's Theory of Cognitive Development.* New York: David McKay, 1971. A concise and readable survey of the main concepts of Piaget, especially on cognitive development as it relates to learning. Chapter 6, "The Period of Formal Operations," is especially relevant to the major thesis of this book.

---

* The author's major references in writing *Making Sense* were Vygotsky's *Thought and Language* and Bruner's *A Study of Thinking*. The bibliography presented here has been kept short and the books cited are general references, many of which include additional excellent bibliographies.

GROUPING

Ability Grouping. Washington, D.C.: National Education Association, 1968. A review of research on grouping leads to a useful summary of the considerations involved in different kinds of grouping.

LANGUAGE AND THOUGHT

Miller, G. (Ed.). *Communication, Language, and Meaning.* New York: Basic Books, 1973. A sound, yet readable, volume written by authorities on different aspects of the field, especially for the general reader. Included are chapters on the realm of syntax, learning to read, and communications and computers. There is an excellent bibliography for each chapter.

O'Hare, F. *Sentence-Combining: Improving Student Writing without Formal Grammar Instruction.* Urbana, Illinois: National Council of Teachers of English, 1973. A brief account of a study with seventh graders. Exercises required the use of specific functions words. Examples are given.

Vygotsky, L. S. *Thought and Language.* Cambridge: Massachusetts Institute of Technology, 1962. Originally published in Russia. Influenced many writers, including Luria and Bruner who wrote the introduction. It is essentially a theory of intellectual development.

LISTENING

Lundsteen, S. W. *Listening: Its Impact On Reading and the Other Language Arts.* Urbana, Illinois: NCTE/ERIC, 1971. A useful monograph explaining what is known to date about listening in this context. It provides practical suggestions, including student checklists.

LOGIC

Ennis, R. H. *Logic in Teaching.* Englewood Cliffs, New Jersey: Prentice-Hall, 1969. A well-organized text with chapter summaries and comprehension self-tests. Covers important aspects of logic as used in teaching.

Mitchell, D. *An Introduction to Logic.* London: Hutchinson University Library, 1962. A well-written book which includes some aspects of logic not covered in the Salmon and Ennis books and a most relevant section on the logic of relations.

Salmon, W. C. *Logic.* Englewood Cliffs, New Jersey: Prentice-Hall, 1973. A very brief, concise paperback intended for those who are interested in understanding the basics of logic. Chapters cover deduction, induction, and logic in language. Examples are carefully chosen.

PERSPECTIVE: THE WAY WE LOOK AT THE WORLD

Arnheim, R.   *Visual Thinking.* Berkeley: University of California Press, 1969. An important paperback of general interest to anyone curious about the interdependence of thinking and seeing.

Bronowski, J.   *The Ascent of Man.* Boston: Little, Brown, 1973. A readable, illustrated book developed from thirteen television programs on the topic. Shows how most of the seminal ideas which profoundly changed our world were new ways of looking at existing phenomena, rather than inventions. Demonstrates how these seminal ideas gradually spread to all areas of life and thought.

Howard, M. (Ed.).   *Imagination: The World of Inner Space.* New York: Scholastic Book Services, 1970. An effective classroom kit for junior high school students, requiring proper introduction by a teacher knowledgeable about imagination and visualization.

QUESTIONING

Carin, A. A., and **R. B. Sund.**   *Developing Questioning Techniques: A Self-Concept Approach.* Columbus, Ohio: Charles E. Merrill, 1971. Includes one chapter based on Bloom's taxonomy and presents a "whole child" approach. Includes good summaries for each chapter, specific suggestions for questioning related to audiovisual materials, and a final chapter on "Evaluating Your Questions."

Sanders, N. M.   *Classroom Questions: What Kinds?* New York: Harper and Row, 1966. Based on Bloom's taxonomy with some reservations, this is a well-organized, well-illustrated, brief, and practical guide to the cognitive aspects of questioning.

READING

Henry, G. H.   *Teaching Reading as Concept Development: Emphasis On Affective Thinking.* Newark, Delaware: International Reading Association, 1974. A book for secondary English teachers which suggests ways of teaching thinking skills through literature. Provides diverse ways of extending the kind of training advocated in *Making Sense.*

Herber, H.   *Teaching Reading in the Content Areas.* Englewood Cliffs, New Jersey: Prentice-Hall, 1970. An influential book advocating the teaching of reading through meaningful content rather than isolated exercises. Most helpful in explaining the reasons for not assuming that pupils have sufficient background information for beginning study.

Stauffer, R. G.   *Teaching Reading as a Thinking Process.* New York: Harper and Row, 1969. College text for elementary teachers, but provides a good introduction to aspects of reading development for secondary teachers. Chapter 8 on "The Language Experience Approach" is especially valuable.

Thomas, E. L., and **H. A. Robinson.** *Improving Reading in Every Class.* Boston: Allyn and Bacon, 1972. A clearly written paperback covering all fields of instruction and providing specific examples.

THE THINKING PROCESS

Bruner, J. S., J. J. Goodnow, and **G. A. Austin.** *A Study of Thinking.* New York: John Wiley and Sons, 1956. First 80 pages thoroughly and readably present the categorizing process and its role in concept attainment.

Bruner, J. S., and **J. M. Anglin** (Eds.). *Beyond the Information Given.* New York: W. W. Norton, 1973. Bruner's writings on the psychology of knowing are presented in useful sections.

Dewey, J. *How We Think.* Boston: Heath, 1933. Still a highly readable and useful book, even though Dewey did not have the advantage of recent research.

Luria, A. R. *The Working Brain: An Introduction to Neuropsychology.* New York: Basic Books, 1973. Presents what is known and what is surmised about the physical workings of the mind. Sections on memory and on the different effects of injuries to particular parts of the brain at different stages of development are especially relevant.